GW01338928

Voyage to Vegetarianism

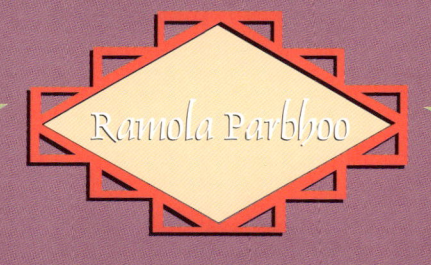

Ramola Parbhoo

© Editions de l'Océan Indien Ltée (1994)
Ramola Parbhoo

Design & layout : Shakuntala Seecharun
Illustrations : Nirmala Luckeenarain
Photographs : Pankaj Shah (India)

Published by
Editions de l'Océan Indien Ltée
Stanley, Rose-Hill
Mauritius

Typesetting: Mauritius Printing Specialists (Pte) Ltd, Mauritius
Printing: SNP Printing Pte Ltd
1st Reprint: SNP Printing Pte Ltd

ISBN 99903-0-135-2

CONTENTS

Introduction	iv
Spices	1
Herbs	6
Hearty soups	9
Garden fresh salads	13
Vegetarian main course	27
Pulses	53
Home baked breads	63
Delectable snacks, savouries and dips	79
Fresh chutneys, pickles and sauces for snacks	87
Irresistible desserts, puddings, ice creams and sweetmeats	93
Eggless cakes and biscuits	107
Fruit juice, punch, milkshake and sherbets	115

INTRODUCTION

Vegetarian cooking reigns supreme in the East. The art is acquired with the special attention and love which the gourmet develops when nurturing delicacies made from homemade bread and cheese, exotic vegetables, saffron, spices, nuts, lentils, rice and yoghurt. With patience any cook can add that touch of class to the vegetarian cuisine.

Vegetarianism was practised thousands of years ago. Hinduism, Buddhism and Jainism propagated this way of life for the enrichment and fulfilment of the mind, body and soul. By the year 269 BC, the reign of Ashoka became a landmark in the development of vegetarianism since he set his own example which was emulated by his people.

Vegetarianism is a trend that is spreading around the world.

"It is in my view that the vegetarian manner of living by its purely physical effect on the human temperament, would most beneficially influence the lot of mankind." Albert Einstein.

Good Nutrition

The correct intake of vitamins and minerals gives us a balanced diet. This balanced diet then supplies all the needs of the body. An adequate and balanced diet is one which provides proteins and minerals which are essential in body building materials, fats and carbohydrates which produce energy and fuel, water, minerals and fibre which act as regulators.

Vitamins

Vital vitamins are found in fresh fruits. Apples, mangoes, grapes and the vitamin C packed-orange and grape fruit can keep us vitamin sufficient. Every vitamin known to be required by our bodies for good health performs a specific function that no other nutrient can perform. Deficiency of just one of these specific substances can have a harmful effect and cause long term illnesses.

Excessive doses of some vitamins can also cause adverse reactions within the body. (Vitamins are essential for chemical reactions throughout the body). Most vitamins cannot be manufactured by the body, so they need to be in the food we eat. Other sources of vitamins are fresh green and yellow vegetables.

Proteins

Proteins are needed to build muscles and maintain the body. Proteins can be found in soya and milk. The main source of protein is lentils. Lentils are as popular and widely used as rice. A variety of pulses, dried beans, split and whole lentils which are packed with high food value, provide the family with a daily measure of protein. A wide selection of menus can be prepared by the imaginative use of these simple lentils. Numerous types are grown everywhere and these are eaten as a dhal or thick gravy, with rice. Certain lentils are sprouted and then prepared into vegetarian delicacies for added proteins.

Extra proteins are provided by the extensive use of milk and yoghurt. Nutritious, spiced milk drinks and raitas are made with yoghurt or homemade curd.

Minerals

These are calcium, phosphorus, zinc, iron, potassium and sodium found in practically all fresh vegetables and fruits. A supplement of calcium may be needed as our bones grow older.

Water

Water is essential to all tissues. A good percentage of our body weight is made up of water. Water is naturally found in all the food we eat. One needs to drink seven to eight glasses of water everyday.

Carbohydrates

Carbohydrates supply energy to the body and are generally lower in calories than fats. These are available in sugars and starches.

- *natural sugars in fresh fruits, vegetables and some dairy products;*
- *pure and refined sugars such as table sugar, brown sugar, honey, molasses;*
- *potatoes, bread, cereals, pasta;*
- *foods that contain natural sugar like fruits, supply not only energy but nutrients such as vitamins.*
- *Rice is combined with almonds, nuts, sugar and milk to produce delicate desserts. Of particular importance is the versatility that rice and lentils have acquired in the vegetarian diet. But above all, rice is still one of nature's abundant, economical and rich nutrients.*

Fats

Fats are concentrated energy, essential for good health and a necessary part of a well balanced diet, even when trying to lose weight. Fats make it possible for your body to use up carbohydrates and proteins. They are a highly concentrated form of energy. Fats are found in butter, margarine and oil. Hidden fats are found in baked products such as cakes, salad dressings, nuts, eggs, milk products and fried foods.

Saturated Fats

These are mostly fats that are solid at room temperature e.g. animal fats and some vegetable fats such as coconut oil.

Unsaturated Fats

These are usually liquid fats, such as sunflower, corn, peanuts and soya bean oil. Polyunsaturated fats are a chemical variation of unsaturated fats. These are usually recommended. The body needs no more than three teaspoons of fat a day.

A selection of spices.

Spices

To travel through India from the ice-caped Himalayas to the subtropical tip of Sri Lanka is to be introduced to the rich diversity of a cuisine which amazes the traveller. Since twenty-five or more spices utilized throughout the land are used in different techniques and with ingredients which are natural to the region, a tantalizing diversity is created from place to place. With the Mogul emperor's invasion four centuries ago, the richness of the Persian culinary tradition was introduced with creamy sauces, spices laden with sweet fragrances of rosé and lime essence. The sweet spices of cardamon, cloves and cinnamon are the secret of rich pilaus decked with kingly saffron from the treasured hills of Kashmir.

Early Indian literature in Sanskrit, from the Vedic period 3000 years ago, emphasises the character and importance of spices particularly for preserving food. The Ayurveda, an ancient Hindu treatise on medicine, places special emphasis on the medical properties of spices.

How to buy, roast, store and crush spices?

Buy in small quantities and store in labelled airtight jars. Select spices which have a strong aroma, when crushed. Fresh spices are always aromatic. Most spices have a twelve-month shelf life. When roasting your own spices you will enhance the quality as well as increase the life as you will dry any moisture which usually affects the strength of a spice.

Pre-heat the oven to 100°C and spread spices on a tray. Leave in the oven for 20 minutes, stirring once. Switch off the oven and allow spices to stand another 15 minutes. Cool and pack in jars which are airtight. For quick roasting a little at a time, place in a dry pan over a low stove and heat for about 2 minutes. Cool and crush. A mortar and pestle, a rolling pin or an electric coffee grinder crushes spices beautifully.

The function of spices

Spices are used for flavouring, for medicinal purposes, for preserving and, most important, spices are used purely for aroma and fragrance. To extract a spice aroma and infuse it into a dish is an art. This technique called the vagaar or bhagaar should precede a dish.

How to create a good vagaar (aroma)?

Use a heavy bottom saucepan with a good fitting lid. Put in a few teaspoons or more of pure ghee or oil. Heat until just smoking then quickly add the spices of your choice. Cover the pot. After 5 seconds add your lentils or vegetables or whatever you are preparing. Cover the lid immediately and lower the heat of your hot plate. The aromas of the selected spices will infuse your food.

Spice List

Ajowan (ajmo) – carum copticum

Ajowan is used as an aromatic for vegetables such as peas, beans and potatoes. Counteracts flatulence, alleviates colic.

Aniseed (Soomph/Varyari) pimpinella anisum

Gives chilli-bites an excellent flavour. In South Africa they are used to flavour vegetable dishes. These elongated green seeds with a taste of liquorice are used as a mouth freshener. 'Anise' is similar to aniseed.

Asafoetida (Hing) – ferula assa – foetida

Digestive, chiefly used in lentil and bean dishes. Buy this spice in powder form since the gum has to be roasted and then pounded to a fine powder. Digestive powders and in the East is an antidote for opium and flatulence. Dried resin is derived from the roots of various plants from western Kashmir, East India and Iran.

Bay Leaves – laurus nobilus

Used for casseroles, soups, pickles, savouries and pate. It is said that bay leaf oil gives relief from rheumatism, sprains and bruises.

Cardamom pods (Elaichi) – elettaria cardamomum

The buff pods are used in rice and sweet dishes.

The distinctive warm flavour can be added to coffee, baked apples and apple pies, cakes and buns.

Chilli (Mircha) – capsicum frutescens

Chillies are the prime ingredient in masalas, giving dishes the necessary heat and flavour. Fresh green chillies contain flat white seeds and have a distinctive flavour. They have considerable vitamin A and C content. The dried red chilli is either used whole in certain dishes to impart a specific aroma, or is ground to a fine powder called cayenne pepper or chilli powder. In some cases the seeds, which provide the heat, are removed from the dried red chilli to reduce the heat of the dish. Powdered chillies are used to neutralise poison and numbness of the body, and to relieve hypothermia in cases of cholera.

Chilli Powder

Ground from small dried red chillies.

Cayenne

Ground from dried chilli which is hotter than any spice and is orange-red in colour.

Paprika

Also ground chillies coming from yet another species.

How to handle chillies

Their volatile oil can make your skin tingle and your eyes burn. Use a pair of rubber gloves, and avoid touching your face or eyes while working.

Try rubbing sunflower oil onto your hands to prevent irritation.

Rinse chillies in cold water. Hot water causes fumes to rise from dried chillies and these may be advisable to work under cold running water when removing the stem of the chilli. Rinse several times.

The flavour is in the fresh pod itself, the seeds are responsible for the heat of the chilli. Use both the pods and the seeds.

Masalas give heat to any dish. If you require less heat, reduce the amount of masala as given in my recipes.

Cinnamon/Cassia – (Tuj) – cinnamomum cassia

An aromatic rice, lentils and vegetables. Ground cinnamon is used for sweet dishes, milk puddings and spicy tea. Added to custard, stews fruits, such as apples, bananas, oranges and prunes.

The more pungent, rougher looking cinnamon sticks are used in Indian cookery. Finely rolled cinamon sticks do not have a strong aroma.

Cloves – (Lavang) – eugenia caryophyllata

Cloves are used for their aromatic qualities. Clove oil is used as a local anaesthetic.

It is a powerfully scented flower bud and is known to alleviate nausea.

Coriander seeds (dhunia) – Coriandrum Sativum

Dhunia seeds are highly aromatic and suggest a lemony or sage flavour. The herb is used extensively in cooking.

In Mexico coriander is known as cilantro *and in Mauritius it is known as* cotomili.

Cumin seeds (Jeero) – cuminum cyminum

Used in most vegetarian dishes. Crushed cumin is an excellent flavouring for fresh chutney, yoghurt drinks, dressings and pineapple salad. It is used also in cakes, apple tarts and fruit puddings. Cumin's strong and aromatic flavour can be added to tomato salads, cheese dishes and dried beans.

Curry Leaves (Limri/Kariyapula) – chalcas koenigii

Flavour South Indian dishes. The pungent leaves are used in potato dishes, also with red lentils or oil lentil dishes.

Fenugreek Seeds (Methi) – trigonella foenumgraecum

Lightly roasted seeds are used for potato and savoury dishes. The herb is used for its bitter flavour, particularly in savouries and pancakes.

Fenugreek gives relief from cough, asthma and rheumatism and strengthen the back. Drink a tea for relief.

Ginger – zingiber officinale

Use the fresh or dried form.

Soak the green ginger in hot water for about 30 minutes before scraping it. Never peel ginger, but scrape it as you would a carrot. Fresh ginger is recognised by its juiciness and the ease with which it is scraped. The younger the root, the more delicate its flavour.

Garlic – allium sativum

Mature garlic bulbs are made of tightly clustered bulbets or cloves. Garlic is indispensable in most cooking. Peel and crush until smooth, make a garlic masala. (See Masalas p.   ).

Mustard Seed (Rai) – brassica nigra

Used in lentil and vegetable dishes. English mustard is made from brown and white mustard seeds which is hot.

Nutmeg (Jaiphul) – myristica fragrams

Grated nutmeg is used to flavour milk and sweet dishes. Grate freshly for maximum flavour. Nutmeg adds a sweet, spicy flavour to vegetables, like sweet potato, pumpkin, cauliflower, cabbage, spinach, carrots, cucumber. Grate over steamed vegetables and season with salt, a sprinkling of sugar and butter.

Nutmeg with warm milk, sugar and almonds make a good sedative as a bedtime drink.

The nutmeg is surrounded by lacy coverings which is mace.

Peppercorns, black or white (Kara mari – dora mari) – piper nigrum

Peppercorns act as a hot garnish.

Poppy Seeds (khas khas) – papauer somniferum

Poppy seeds make a delectable vegetarian dish when cooked. Use with breads, biscuits, cakes, salads, noodles and vegetables.

Saffron (Kesar) – crocus sativus

Saffron is the most expensive spice in the world. Grown in the lofty Himalayas and other mountainous areas. A single strand of saffron comes from a crocus flower, making saffron extremely expensive. Saffron is usually soaked in warm water or milk to extract its brilliant yellow pigment. Saffron also contributes a mildly bitter flavour and is used in most of the exotic rice dishes of India, such as biryani, pilau and certain delectable sweet dishes. A few of the dried filaments (approximately half a teaspoon) will give flavour and colour to an average sized dish. 75,000 strands make 1kg – hence the cost factor.

Sesame seeds (Til) – sesmum indicum

Used in many sweets and vegetables savouries. Small beige unhulled seeds, highly nutritious and with a nutty flavour, especially when roasted.

Tamarind (Imli) – tamarindus indica

The dried seed pod is soaked in warm water to extract its acidic watery pulp. The pulp is especially used in southern India, where it is valued for its acid yet sweet taste. Preferable to vinegar wherever tartness or piquancy is required.

Turmeric (Halud/Arad) – curcuma longa

Turmeric is the dried fleshy rhizome of a perennial plant belonging to the ginger family. When fresh, the roots resemble ginger but are yellow. Turmeric's bright yellow pigment is used for colouring. Its earthy, pungent flavour may overwhelm and ruin the dish. Used in ground form, as a powder. Use in small quantities because of its brilliance and bitter taste.

Vanilla

Vanilla pods are used for flavouring sweets and cakes in the form of vanilla sugar. Vanilla essence is an essential flavouring for baking.

Blends of Spices – Masalas

Masala is a mixture of the principal ingredients necessary for any particular dish. It can either be made of fresh ingredients such as chillies, ginger and garlic, or from dried roasted spices.

Grind the spices from the whole seeds, taking a little time and trouble to obtain the subtle and freshness which only home grinding gives to your dishes. Use a blender, processor, mincer, electric food grinder or a simple mortar and pestle to grind masalas.

Green Masala Blend

500 g green chillies
400 g garlic cloves
400 g ginger
4 T salt
6 T cooking oil
1/2 T turmeric

Method

Protect your fingers and wash the chillies.

Peel the garlic and scrape the skin off the ginger.

Pound to paste with a mortar and pestle, the traditional Indian method, or use a food processor, or a small blender or liquidiser.

Place chillies, garlic and ginger in the machine.

Add the oil so that the machine has some liquid.

Process to a fine paste.

Remove and mix with salt and turmeric.

To Store

The turmeric, salt and oil mixture acts as a preservative, enabling the masala to be kept for 2 to 8 weeks in the refrigerator. Store in a glass jar with a closely fitting lid.

Freezing any excess is a good way of keeping masala almost indefinitely. Storing reduces the fresh flavour of chillies, but not their heat. The storing of masalas is convenient for people who have only limited time for cooking.

Uses

Besides making food chilli-hot, green masala adds a fresh chilli taste to any dish.

Red Masala Blend

Red Masala is far hotter than green masala.

500 g red dried chillies
500 g garlic cloves
500 g ginger (root)
4 T salt
6 T cooking oil

Method

Protect your fingers and follow the same method as for green masala, adding the water to mix. Store in a glass jar, covering the masala with 4 tsp oil.

Red masala imparts an attractive reddish colour and is often used for lentil dishes.

Gharam Masala

A final spicing to enhance dishes. Seldom used in the initial stages of any dish.

10 g tuj/cinnamon sticks
10 g elaichi/whole cardamon pods, preferably green
10 g lavang/cloves
20 g jeera/cumin seeds
30 g dhunia/coriander seeds
30 g whole black peppercorns

Method

Open the cardamons pods to remove the seeds. Break the cinnamon into small pieces. Roast spices in oven for 30 minutes but do not allow to brown. Grind the spices in a coffee grinder to make a very smooth powder.

Dhunia Jeera Masala (Coriander/Cumin Masala)

An essentially Gujerati spice mixture, used exclusively for vegetarian dishes.

100 g dhunia/coriander seeds
50 g jeera / cumin seeds

Method

Follow instructions for roasting spices. Place the roasted seeds in an electric blender and blend at a high speed for 2-3 minutes until you obtain a coarse powder. Store in a jar.

Root Ginger Masala

200 g fresh root ginger
45 ml (3T) cooking oil
30 ml (2T) salt
60 ml (4T) water

Method

Soak the ginger, then scrape and chop into convenient pieces. Place in a food processor or liquidiser and reduce to a smooth paste, adding the oil and water.
Lastly, mix in the salt.

Keep in a close glass jar for up to 8 weeks in the refrigerator. Ginger paste freezes beautifully for up to 6 months.

Garlic Masala

200 g garlic cloves
30 ml (2T) salt
45 ml (3T) cooking oil

Method

Garlic gives off a strong oil which may cause a burning sensation. Rub the tips of your fingers with cooking oil to form a barrier. Soak the cloves of garlic in hot water for 30 minutes, to loosen the skins and make peeling easier.

Place garlic, salt and oil in a blender and reduce to a paste, or use a mortar and pestle.

Keep in a glass screw top jar in the refrigerator for up to 8 weeks. The paste may also be frozen for up to 6 months.

Other Important Ingredients

Ghee

Ghee *is considered to be a pure food in the East. It enhances* sattwic *(good) qualities in one and is offered to the Gods at sacrificial fires as the purest offering. A ghee lamp lights every Hindu home and signifies the light which dispels darkness and evil. Ghee is an ingredient that cannot be substituted, for its flavour is unique.*

Ghee *is butter in a clarified form suitable for using in* vagaars *(a technique) where the butter has to be heated to a high temperature – otherwise ordinary butter would burn. For the same reason,* ghee *also makes frying less troublesome. Many Indian sweet dishes are enhanced by gently frying in* ghee. *Another important advantage is that ghee can be stored at room temperature for over twelve months, – perfect for camping or outdoor cooking.*

How to make ghee

Place 500g butter in a deep saucepan and bring to a gentle boil. Keep at a low to medium temperature and boil the liquid butter slowly for 10-15 minutes. You will hear a bubbling sound until all the water has evaporated from the ghee. At this stage a layer of scum will rise to the surface, the salt will settle at the bottom and the clarified butter will remain in the middle. Place another container on a surface nearby with a cotton cloth on top. Remove the ghee *from the heat and blow the scum to one side of the saucepan. Pour the clarified butter into the container, leaving the salt at the bottom of the saucepan. The ghee should be crystal clear.*

To store

Cool and store in a steel, enamel or glass container.

Note : Never leave ghee *unattended on the stove: it may boil over and catch alight. Keep children well away.*

Herbs

The cultivation of one's own herb garden can be a most rewarding and pleasurable pursuit. Herbs are not demanding and need very little time and space. A herb garden can even be contained in a large pot on a window ledge. Herbs lend flavour, fragrance and beauty to food and possess a magical subtlety that has to be savoured. Health scientists are discovering more and more uses of these delicate plants and are propagating their rightful benefits. Chopped herbs can be combined with salads, soups, butter, cream fillings and breads. Garden fresh herbs have found their niche in every spectrum of cooking.

Herbs in Indian Cooking

Coriander Herb (Dhunia) – coriandrum sativum

The principal garnish for most indian dishes. A pungent aromatic herb of the parsley family, also known as cilantro – *used in Mexican cooking.*

To store : Buy dhunia *in small bunches, remove the roots and store in an airtight container in the refrigerator. Avoid wetting the leaves. Alternatively, place in a damp kitchen towel or damp brown paper and store in the fridge for about 1 week.*

To freeze : Wash clean and chop finely, place in an ice-cube tray with a little water and freeze, use the ice-cubes for cooking.

To dry : leave in the sun until crisp and pound to a powder.

To clean : Remove the roots and soak in plenty of cold water for about 15 minutes. Rinse the herb several times. Chop both stems and leaves finely.

To grow : Buy coriander seeds for planting, crush lightly and spread on damp fertile soil. Cover lightly with soil. Choose a warm spot, avoiding intense direct sunlight.

Fenugreek Herb (methi bhaji) – trigonella foenumgraecum

Has a strong bitter flavour and aroma. Use the leaves and only the softer portions of the stem.

For storing, use the same method as for dhunia. *It is valuable for convalescents because of its remedial qualities.*

Mint (Poodina/foodina) mentha spicata

Garden mint or spearmint is used frequently as a garnish. Apple mint, penny royal and peppermint are also used to flavour spiced tea. Lemon mint and basil mint make delicious teas.

Basil (Tulsi)

In the East the basil is worshipped as the holy tulsi. Being a sacred plant in the Hindu context the tulsi is cultivated in most gardens. Basil acts as a prophylactic against malaria, being a valuable remedy for colds and coughs.

Use leaves with pastas, soups, pea soups, salads, sliced pineapples, sliced cucumbers, cream cheese dips, sandwich fillings and tomato based sauces.

Garlic Chives

Give a delicate garlic hint to dishes. Add attractive greenery to salads and vegetables. Chop chives and use in soups, pizzas and savouries.

Onion Chives

These onion flavoured chives contain a pungent oil which stimulates the appetite. It is said to lower high blood pressure. A source of calcium which keeps the bones, teeth and nails strong.

Other Popular Herbs

Water Cress

Has a peppery flavour and is a wonderful source of nutrients as fresh salad. Water cress soup is excellent.

Dill

Dill is a soothing herb well known to the ancient people. The seeds are rich in oil and used to flavour cabbage, cucumber, pickles, bread and cooked vegetables.

Used as a garnish when finely chopped.

Fennel

Fennel is valuable for its stem, foliage and seeds in cooking. Used sparingly in potato salads, soups, sauces and green salads. Fennel seeds are good for digestion.

Sweet Marjoram and Oregano

Marjoram is very aromatic, used in the traditional mixed spices. Oregano is very similar and both can be used to top pizza, rice pasta and salads.

Parsley

The curled parsley is used for garnishing. Italian parsley is tall. It imparts an earthy taste to soups, pasta and mashed potatoes. It helps blood circulation, assists the kidney and is said to be just the correct tea for arthritis patients. Rich in vitamins A, B and C and in iron.

Rosemary

Is not just a lovely name and according to Shakespeare, rosemary is good for memory. Grown in the warm Mediterranean climate, it has a pungent flavour which enhances dried beans, chickpeas, lentils, cabbage and brinjals. Rosemary tea can be sipped for improving memory; it is said to "cure forgetfulness and relieve heartaches".

Sage

The shapely sage, in China, is vital as a tonic for the brain to restore energy and vitality. Cooked with onion it is delicious. It imparts a richness to sauces, cheese dishes, green pea soups and breads. It has antiseptic properties.

Tarragon

Tarragon has essential oils which keeps the body warm and is known for its unique and spicy flavour. Salad dressings, mayonnaise, herb vinegars are also enhanced by fresh tarragon.

Thyme

Garden thyme and lemon thyme make casseroles, stews and soups tasty. Mix thyme into bread roll dough, herb butter, dried beans lentil dishes, haricot beans, squash and marrows. Sprinkle over tomatoes and salads. Lemon thyme is milder, used as an antiseptic. Herbalists recommend thyme often as a nerve tonic.

A potato salad which is served warm in Switzerland with a cream tomato soup.

Hearty Soups

Hearty vegetable soup
Tomato and green pepper soup
Lettuce soup
Cauliflower soup
Spinach soup
Pumpkin soup
Tomato soup
Hot Mexican corn soup
Sour soup with mushrooms
(tom yam het - Indonesian style)
Watercress soup
(Bouillon cresson - Mauritian style)

HEARTY VEGETABLE SOUP

Serves 6 — Time : 60 mins

500 g fresh vegetables : pumpkin, potatoes, green beans sliced, carrots, turnips, celery

375 ml (1 1/2 c) pink lentils
1 large onion, finely chopped or grated
30 ml (2 T) butter or ghee
15ml (1 T) lemon juice
125 ml (1/2 c) fresh herbs – parsley and dhunia, chopped
5 ml (1 t) turmeric
4 cloves of garlic, chopped
5 ml (1 t) crushed ginger
5 ml (1 t) freshly ground black pepper OR
5 ml (1 t) red chilli powder
5 ml (1 t) salt, more to taste

Dice vegetables and wash well.
Drain and leave aside.
In a large pot, heat ghee and sauté onions until golden in colour.
Add ginger, garlic, turmeric and salt.
Fry for a minute.
Add vegetables and washed lentils with four cups of warm water.
Cover pot and gently simmer for 45 minutes.
Add fresh herbs and lemon juice.
Cook for 10 minutes.
Serve hot in bowls with homemade bread.

TOMATO AND GREEN PEPPER SOUP

Serves 4 — Time : 20 mins

Vegetables: Tomatoes, green peppers (cheese) coriander herbs/cilantro

2 t vegetable oil
4 large tomatoes, steeped in hot water and peeled
2 medium green peppers seeded and cut into strips
2 1/2 cups vegetable stock or water
397 ml evaporated milk
Hot pepper seasoning in liquid form (Tobasco)
Salt to taste
200 g cheese diced
4 t chopped coriander herb/cilantro

Heat oil in frying pan over medium heat.
Add peppers and tomatoes to pan and fry until peppers are limp.
Pour the vegetable stock into the pan and allow to simmer for 10 minutes, keeping the pan uncovered.
Mix in the milk and add the hot pepper seasoning and salt.
Add cheese, mix and serve immediately.
Garnish with coriander herbs, chopped.

Cilantro or Coriander in Mexican cooking is as widely used as in Asian cooking

LETTUCE SOUP

| Serves 4 | Time : 40 mins |

500 g lettuce leaves
4 cups water
1 t salt
1 t vegetable stock (Optional)
1 t pepper
250 ml cream

Place lettuce, water, salt, vegetable stock and pepper into a pot and boil.

When the lettuce leaves are cooked and soft remove the lettuce and remaining water and liquidise.

Stir the cream into the liquidised mixture and serve.

Variations

Substitute one of the following instead of lettuce.

CAULIFLOWER SOUP

1 small cauliflower

SPINACH SOUP

500 g spinach leaves

PUMPKIN SOUP

500 g peeled pumpkin
Add the juice of 1 orange (1/2 c)
2 t crushed coriander seeds + 1 chopped onion

TOMATO SOUP

500 g tomatoes
Add 2 t sugar

HOT MEXICAN CORN SOUP

| Serves 4 | Time : 30 mins |

750 g whole kernel corn
2 T butter or margarine
2 cups seeded and diced green pepper
1 dry red chilli
1/4 t chilli powder
1/2 t garlic crushed
1/2 t ginger crushed
6 cups vegetable stock or water
1 t salt
1 cup cream

Melt butter and add chilli powder, garlic, ginger and green pepper.

Cook, while stirring, over medium heat in an uncovered pot for 3 minutes.

Add red pepper, corn and vegetable stock.

Bring to the boil.

Simmer for 3 minutes at reduced heat.

Add salt to taste and remove red chilli.

Whip cream and 1/4t salt until stiff.

Pour soup into bowl and top with cream.

When serving soup ladle from bottom of bowl after stirring.

Fresh corn may be cut off the cob and used in this recipe.

SOUR SOUP WITH MUSHROOMS – TOM YAM HET – *Indonesian Style*

Serves 4 — Time : 40 mins

500 g fresh mushrooms, cut
2 lemon grass stalks, sliced
3 fresh lemon leaves
Fresh coriander leaves, chopped
3 red chillies, sliced lengthwise
Juice of 1 lemon
200 g fine dessicated coconut (to make 1 litre coconut milk)
1 1/2 T fish sauce

Boil coconut milk.

Add mushrooms, lemon grass, lemon leaves and fish sauce.

Set heat to medium low.

When mushrooms are done add chillies and simmer for 5 minutes.

Add coriander, lemon juice.

Serve garnished with coriander leaves.

WATERCRESS SOUP – BOUILLON CRESSON – *Mauritian Style*

Serves 4-6 — Time : 30 mins

1 large bunch watercress
1 litre water
1 t garlic crushed
1/2 t ginger crushed
1 t oil
1 t green chilli
Salt to taste
2 chopped tomatoes

Clean watercress and remove thicker stalks and cut into 3 lengths.

Place all ingredients into deep pot and boil for 30 mins.

Serve before or after meals as an appetizer.

A nourishing broth.

Garden fresh Salads

Salad dressings
Aubergine raita
Cheesy raita
Khakadi tamati raita
(tomato and cucumber raita)
Potato raita
Carrot raita
Banana raita
Tomato and onion raita
Banana salad - Malay style - Cape Peninsula
Nepal potato salad
Swiss potato salad
Greek salad
Italian pasta salad
Russian salad
Florida orange salad
Avocado and pawpaw salad - Mexican style
Kachoomer salat - Onion and tomato salad
Gajar salat - carrot salad
Beetroot salad
Kidney bean salad
Mexican orange salad
A useful salad chart

A continental table. Greek salad and Dutch pumpkin soup in the forefront. Italian salad. Deep fried onion rings, mushrooms and sprouted chickpeas, mung and bean sprouts.

SALAD DRESSINGS

DRESSINGS	MIX FOLLOWING INGREDIENTS
Sour Cream	1 c sour cream Salt and pepper to taste 1 t lemon juice 1/4 c chopped chives
Honey and herb	4 T honey 2 T lemon juice 3 T olive oil Salt and pepper 1 T chopped herbs
Herb French Dressing	1 t chopped garlic 1 T chopped watercress 1 T chopped chives 1 T chopped mint 1 t dried mixed herbs 1/4 c wine vinegar 3/4 c olive oil Salt and black pepper to taste
Nuts and yoghurt	1 c plain yoghurt 1/2 T honey 2 T chopped walnuts
Mint and yoghurt	1 c yoghurt 2 t sugar 1 T chopped mint 1 T cream
Spicy yoghurt	1 c yoghurt 1/4 t chopped green chilli 1 t crushed cumin 1/4 t salt 1 t sugar 1 T chopped coriander
Orange and lemon juice	3/4 c orange juice 2 T lemon juice 2 t crushed cumin 2 t sugar 1/2 t salt 3 T olive oil
Cream cheese	125 g cream cheese 2 t sugar 2 T lemon juice 1 T milk 2 T grated cheddar cheese 1/2 t black pepper Salt to taste
Mint dressing	12 fresh mint leaves, finely chopped OR 5 ml (1 t) dried mint 2 ml (1/2 t) crushed cumin 1 clove garlic, peeled and finely crushed 2 ml (1/2 t) salt 5 ml (1 t) sugar 30 ml (2 T) vinegar 60 ml (4 T) salad oil or olive oil

Indian Salad Accompaniments

AUBERGINE RAITA

Serves 4-6 | Time : 15-20 mins

2 brinjals sliced into thin rings
1/2 t salt
2 green chillies, chopped finely
1 t ginger crushed
1/3 cup ghee or oil
500 ml (2 c) yoghurt
1 t crushed garlic
1 t crushed cumin

Sprinkle some of the salt over the brinjal rings.
Make a paste with the chillies and ginger and spread onto the brinjal.
Fry the brinjal in the ghee until crispy.
Mix the garlic, cumin and salt with the yoghurt.
Place in a bowl and put the brinjal crisps on top of the yoghurt.
Chill and serve as a salad.

CHEESY RAITA

Serves 4 | Time : 15 mins

500 ml (2 c) yoghurt
1/2 t salt
2 T cheddar cheese, finely grated
1 finely chopped tomato
1 finely chopped onion
125 ml finely chopped cucumber
1/2 t black pepper powder
1 t cumin powder
1 sliced green chilli
1 t chilli powder

Mix yoghurt with salt.
Add the cheese, the vegetables and mix.
Sprinkle the black pepper, cumin and chilli powder over the salad.

This yoghurt is served chilled as an accompaniment to any pilau.

KHAKADI TAMATI RAITA – (TOMATO AND CUCUMBER RAITA)

Serves 4-6 | Time : 15 mins

1 cucumber
2 tomatoes
500 ml (2 c) yoghurt
15 ml (1 T) onions, chopped
1 green chilli, chopped
5 ml (1 t) salt
15 ml (1 T) nuts
2 sprigs of coriander leaves, coarsely chopped

Peel and dice cucumber and chop tomatoes.
Place yoghurt into a shallow serving bowl and blend with onions, chillies and salt.
Mix cucumber and tomatoes with yoghurt.
Top with nuts and garnish with coriander sprigs.

Cool cucumbers with yoghurt never fail to cool down a hot palate. Serve with rice dishes.

POTATO RAITA

Serves 4 | Time : 15 mins

250 g potatoes
500 ml (2 c) yoghurt
1/2 t salt
1/2 t chilli powder
2 ml (1/2 t) ground cumin
30 ml (2 T) jaggery or brown sugar
125 ml (1/2 c) tamarind water

Cook, peel and chop the potatoes.
Mix the potatoes, yoghurt and salt together.
Combine the rest of the ingredients together and heat until the sauce becomes thick.
Chill both mixtures and serve together.

CARROT *RAITA*

| Serves 4 | Time : 15 mins |

2 grated carrots
1 sliced green chilli
500 ml (2 c) yoghurt
30 ml (2 T) coriander leaves, chopped
30 ml (2 T) crushed nuts
Salt to taste
5 ml (1 t) crushed cumin

Combine all the ingredients.

BANANA *RAITA*

| Serves 4 | Time : 15 mins |

30 ml (2 T) ghee
5 ml (1 t) mustard seeds
15 ml (1 T) sultanas
500 ml (2 c) yoghurt
2 sliced ripe bananas
2 ml (1/2 t) chilli powder
5 ml (1 t) gharam masala
5 ml (1 t) sugar

Fry the mustard seeds and the sultanas in ghee until the mustard seeds splutter.

Pour the ghee off and combine with other ingredients.

TOMATO AND ONION *RAITA*

| Serves 4 | Time : 15 mins |

15 ml (1 T) ghee
5 ml (1 t) mustard seeds
2 chopped tomatoes
4 sliced spring onions
Some curry leaves
A tiny piece of ginger, chopped finely
1 sliced green chilli
500 ml (2 c) yoghurt
2 T fresh coriander leaves, chopped

Fry mustard seeds in hot ghee until they splutter.
Add the tomatoes, onions and spices.
Cook until the onions turn golden brown.
Mix with the yoghurt and garnish with coriander leaves.

BANANA SALAD – (*Malay style – Cape Peninsula , S. Africa*)

| Serves 6 | Time : 15 mins |

4 large ripe bananas
60 ml (4 T) mayonnaise or salad cream
1T smooth apricot jam or golden syrup
A handful of nuts for decorating
Squeeze of lemon juice
A pinch of cayenne pepper
Few crisp lettuce leaves for presentation

Peel and slice bananas to 5mm thickness.
Mix well with mayonnaise and jam.
Arrange lettuce leaves on platter.
Scoop over banana salad.
Squeeze a tiny bit of lemon juice to prevent discolouring.
Sprinkle with nuts and cayenne pepper.
Served chilled.

Bananas are nature's energy food, containing large amounts of vitamins, minerals and especially rich in potassium.

Where bananas are bountiful in the warm tropical climates, why not make the most of this versatile fruit?

As an easy salad it lends an interesting addition to the vast selection from the valley of salads.

A delicious salad for a light lunch, served with your favourite protein dish.

NEPAL POTATO SALAD

| Serves 6 | ⌚ Time : 20 mins |

500 g boiled potatoes
100 g roasted sesame seeds or peanuts, ground finely
20 ml (4 t) lemon juice
5 ml (1 t) chilli powder
5 ml (1 t) salt
45 ml (3 T) chopped fresh coriander
125 ml (1/2 c) oil
5 ml (1 t) fenugreek seeds

Cook, peel and cube the potatoes.

Add the ground peanuts or sesame seeds, lemon juice, chilli powder, salt and chopped coriander to the cubed potatoes and mix.

Do not mash the potatoes.

Heat the oil in a pan, add the fenugreek and fry for a few seconds.

Add the potato mixture and fry for a few minutes.

Do not allow the mixture to burn.

Serve cool as a delicious salad for any meal.

A superbly flavoured potato salad.

SWISS POTATO SALAD

| Serves 6 | ⌚ Time : 20 mins |

500 g potatoes, boiled in salted water
100 g onions, sliced
1/2 green pepper, cored and sliced
22 ml (1 1/2 T) vinegar
15 ml (1 T) sugar
5 ml (1 t) thyme
15 ml (1 T) salad oil
5 ml (1 t) crushed garlic

Slice potatoes thickly into circles. Keep warm.

Mix in onion, pepper and season with the rest of the ingredients.

Rub some extra garlic into an oven proof bowl.

Top with potato salad.

Serve warm with crusty bread, gherkins, olives, pickled onions and slices of swiss cheese.

A hot salad from the villages of the Swiss Alps.

GREEK SALAD – TYPICAL SALAD OF THE GREEK ISLES

Serves 6 — Time : 15 mins

1 lettuce head, washed and torn into pieces
2 tomatoes, cut into wedges
1 large onion, cut into rings, wash and drain
2 stalks celery, cut into pieces
6 sticks of cucumber
60 ml (1/4 c) pitted black olives
200 g feta cheese, cut into 15mm cubes
3 cloves garlic, crushed or finely chopped

Dressing

60 ml (1/4 c) olive oil
5 ml (1 t) salt
30 ml (2 T) lemon juice
15 ml (1 T) white vinegar

Rub crushed garlic inside wooden bowl.
Arrange salad.
Pour over dressing and serve.

ITALIAN PASTA SALAD

Serves 6 — Time : 20 mins

250 g macaroni, boil in salted water
30 ml (2 T) salad oil
250 ml (1 C) frozen peas, steamed
30 ml (2 T) parsley, chopped
250 ml (1 C) salad cream or Bulgarian yoghurt with 2 ml (1/2 t) salt
30 ml (2 T) chopped parsley

Once macaroni has been boiled, drain and rub salad oil over.
Mix in peas and parsley and cover well with salad cream.
Serve chilled.

RUSSIAN SALAD

Serves 6 — Time : 20 mins

500 ml (2 C) cooked diced potato
250 ml (1 C) cooked diced carrot
250 ml (1 C) cooked diced beetroot
60 ml (1/4 C) roasted cashew nuts
4 ml (1/4 T) tarragon
15 ml (1 T) chives, chopped
15 ml (1 T) parsley, chopped
250 ml (1 C) salad cream
A bed of green salad, e.g. lettuce, watercress

Toss potato, carrots, beetroot with herbs, salt to taste and salad cream.
Layer green salad on plate.
Pile Russian salad over and top with cashew nuts.

FLORIDA ORANGE SALAD

Serves 4 — Time : 15 mins

4 large oranges, peeled and sliced
1 large onion, sliced
1/4 cup grape vinegar
3 T salad oil
1/2 t salt
1 t sugar
Fresh lettuce leaves, shredded
Black pitted olives
A touch of paprika

Place shredded lettuce on a serving platter.
Arrange onion and orange slices in alternate layers.
Mix the vinegar, oil, salt and sugar.
Pour mixture over salad.
Garnish with olives.
Sprinkle with paprika and serve chilled.

A tangy salad from the swinging Florida (USA)

AVOCADO AND PAWPAW SALAD –
Mexican Style

Serves 4 | Time : 20 mins

4 lettuce leaves torn and shredded
2 avocados sliced and seasoned with salt and lemon juice
4 slices pawpaw
6 olives
8 tomatoes wedges
8 carrot sticks
Salt to taste
1/4 t mustard powder

Put lettuce into bowl and arrange avocado and pawpaw slices on the lettuce.

Garnish with olives, tomato wedges and carrot sticks.

Sprinkle with salt and mustard.

Serve with mayonnaise or french dressing.

Serve chilled.

KACHOOMER SALAT – ONION AND TOMATO SALAD

Serves 4-6 | Time : 15 mins

2 onions
2 ripe tomatoes
1 green pepper
2 ml (1/2 t) salt
1/2 green chilli, chopped finely – optional
2 ml (1/2 t) cumin, crushed
2 ml (1/2 t) sugar
15 ml (1 T) lemon juice
15 ml (1 T) vinegar
2 sprigs of coriander or any green dressing
e.g. mint, shallot

Dice onions, tomatoes and green pepper.

Season with salt, chillies, cumin, sugar, lemon juice and vinegar.

Mix well and garnish with sprigs of coriander.

Serve cold.

A traditional Indian salad served with main dishes. Most salads are seasoned, before serving, with chillies, cumin and vinegar.

GAJAR SALAT – CARROT SALAD

Serves 4 — Time : 20 mins

250 g carrots, diced into pieces
15 ml (1 T) ghee
5 ml (1 t) mustard seeds
5 ml (1 t) lemon juice
5 ml (1 t) sugar
5 ml (1 t) chilli powder
5 ml (1 t) salt

Heat ghee in a saucepan.

Place the mustard seeds into ghee and cook until they splutter.

Put the carrots and some water into the pan and cook until carrots are soft.

Mix lemon juice, chilli powder, sugar and salt.

This salad can be served cold or hot. Excellent for rice and lentil dishes.

BEETROOT SALAD

Serves 4 — Time : 60 mins

2 beetroots
1 chopped tomato
1 sliced green chilli
2 T chopped spring onions
1 T lemon juice
1 t sugar
1 t salt

Cook the beetroots until done.

Cut beetroots into cubes.

Combine with the tomato, chilli and the spring onions.

Sprinkle lemon juice, sugar and salt over the salad.

KIDNEY BEAN SALAD

Serves 4 — Time : 15 mins

1 large tin kidney beans
1/2 onion chopped
2 cups celery chopped
4 small gherkins or pickles chopped
1/2 cup walnuts chopped
3 T grape vinegar
1/4 cup vegetable oil
1/2 t salt
1/2 t pepper
1 large lettuce

Drain beans.

Mix with onion, celery, pickles and nuts.

Combine vinegar, oil, pepper and salt.

Combine sauce and bean mixture and refrigerate.

Place lettuce leaves in cold water for 15 minutes to crispen.

Serve salad on leaves in individual salad plates.

MEXICAN ORANGE SALAD

Serves 4 — Time : 15 mins

4 large oranges, peeled and sliced
1 large onion, sliced
1/4 cup grape vinegar
3 T salad oil
1/2 t salt
1/4 t chilli powder
1 t sugar
Fresh lettuce leaves, shredded
Black pitted olives
A touch of paprika

Place shredded lettuce on a serving platter.

Arrange onion and orange slices in alternate layers.

Mix the vinegar, oil, salt, chilli powder and sugar.

Pour mixture over salad.

Garnish with olives.

Sprinkle with paprika and serve chilled.

A tangy salad from the Mexican highlands.

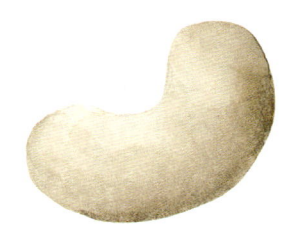

A Useful Salad Chart

Salad	Quantity and Preparations	Combined With	Herbs and Spices	Seasonings and Dressings	Presentation and Serving Suggestions	Nutrients Values and Tips
Apple salad	Grate 3 apples with skin or without. To avoid discolouring squeeze lemon juice over.	Add 2 t sultanas, 2 t peanuts, crushed coarsely and mix with the rest.	Chop 1 sprig of parsley or mint. Add a pinch of chilli powder.	1/2 t salt 1/2 t honey	Individual salad bowls. Garnish with very thin apple slices with red or green skins. Serves 4.	Fibre, vitamins from apples. Apples are economical health lunch.
Apples, carrots and pineapples	Grate 2 apples, 2 carrots, chop 1/2 C pineapple.	Add 1/2 C chopped walnuts.	Chop 1 sprig of parsley or 1 t coriander leaves.	1/2 t salt, 1 t honey, 1/2 C fresh orange juice or juice of 1 orange.	Serve in a large glass bowl. Cut 2 pineapples horizontally leaving the green top. Scoop out flesh for salad and use to fill.	Carrots contain Vitamin A and Carotene.
Apple and cottage cheese	Grate 1 apple.	1 C cottage cheese, 2 t sour cream or 1 T milk.	Chop 2 t thyme, 2 cloves of garlic chopped, 1 t freshly ground black pepper.	1/2 t salt	Serve on individual platters lined with a fresh lettuce leaf and push a few savoury biscuits onto the piled cheese. Sprinkle a tiny pinch of red chilli powder on top to colour.	Cheese is an excellent protein. Garlic is a health preserving.
Asparagus	Wash, remove 3 cm from base of stalk. Tie in bundle + stand in saucepan of salted water. Cook for 25 mins.	Asparagus in tins can be used in tossed salads; as toppings on snack biscuits.		Sprinkle a pinch of cayenne pepper for colour.	Asparagus can be served on a plate on its own topped with fresh herbs as a garnish.	Vitamin A, C, Calcium Phosphorus, Potassium and Iron.
Avocado	Serves 2 Peel and slice 1 ripe avocado pear.	Squeeze on lemon juice to prevent discolouring.	Chop a sprig of rosemary.	Salt and black pepper.	Serve on toast, as a snack, with cottage cheese for sandwiches. Sprinkle with sugar as a dessert.	Rich in vitamins, Proteins. Avocado makes thick milkshake. Combine 1 C milk with 1/2 ripe avocado and sugar to taste.
Beetroot and onion	Serves 4 Boil 4 beetroots peel and slice.	Slice 2 onions, wash well and drain.	Chop 2 t green onion.	1 t salt, 2 t sugar, 2 T brown vinegar.	Serve in glass bowl on a bed of lettuce leaves. Garnish with green onion.	Beetroot preserves well. Stays fresh in fridge for 1 week.
Beetroot and rice	Serves 4 Boil 4 beetroots peel and grate.	Add 1 cup cooked brown rice.	2 t chopped coriander herb.	1 t salt, 2 t sugar, 2 T salad cream.	Serve in wooden salad bowl. Sprinkle chopped herbs.	Beetroot for Potassium tops have Iron + Vit A.

Salad	Quantity and Preparations	Combined With	Herbs and Spices	Seasonings and Dressings	Presentation and Serving Suggestions	Nutrients Values and Tips
Beetroot and potato	Serves 4. Boil 4 beetroots peel and cube.	Add 1 C boiled cubed potato.	2 t chopped parsley.	3 T salad cream or 4 T sour cream, 1 1/2 t salt, pepper to taste.	Serve in a potted bowl. Decorate with sprigs of parsley on top.	Potatoes for Vitamin C Phosphorus and Potassium.
Beans	Serves 6. Soak 1 1/2 c of dried beans. e.g. haricot, lady beans. Boil until cooked in unsalted water.	Fry 2 large onions, sliced in 3 T oil until brown and kidney with drained beans.	Add 3 T chopped herbs. e.g. thyme 1 t 1 T roasted sesame seeds. 1 T chilli powder. Mix well.	1 T vinegar 1 t sugar 2 t salt	Line a deep glass bowl with cabbage leaves. Pile beans to the top. Sprinkle with sesame seeds and herbs.	Beans are rich in Vitamin A.
Baked beans	Serves 2. 420g tin baked beans.	Add 2 T chopped green pepper 3 T chopped onion.	1 T chopped parsley or coriander.	1/2 chopped green chilli	Garnish with rings of green and red pepper.	As above.
Green beans.	Serves 4 500 g green beans steamed till cooked.	2 onions. Fry with 2 T crushed sesame seeds in 3 T salad oil.	1 t chilli powder. 1t chopped coriander.	1 t salt black pepper 3 T vinegar	Excellent for **braais*** and cold lunches.	As above.
Broccoli	Serves 4 Steam 400 g till cooked.	Steam 100 g cauliflower. Add 2 T butter.	1 T chopped rosemary or 2 T chopped coriander herb.	Toss with 4 T salad dressing. Season with salt.	Chop 2 t garlic finely and rub into a large salad bowl. Fill with salad.	Broccoli contains Vit A, B, B_2, C Calcium and Iron.
Brinjal	Serves 4 Choose young brinjal. Slice with skin on. Sprinkle with salt. Pat brinjal dry.	Heat 4 T oil in pan and fry brinjal on both sides until brown.	Chop 2 T coriander leaves. Sprinkle 1/2 t red chilli powder, 1 t crushed cumin.	Whip 1/2 C fresh cream into 1 C of yoghurt. Season with 1/2 t salt and black pepper.	Place yoghurt in a flat bowl. Arrange fried brinjal over and garnish with herb and a sprinkle of chilli powder.	Brinjals are low in kilojoules. Contains Calcium, Magnesium and Potassium.
Cabbage	Serves 6. Chop 1/2 head or 3 C cabbage chopped.	1 apple cubed 2 t sultanas 1 grated carrot.	Chop 2 t fresh herbs	Add 2 t sugar 1t salt 1/2 c salad cream or yoghurt.	line a bowl with fresh cabbage leaves and pile salad to top.	Contains Vit A, C, Calcium, Phosphorus and Potassium.
Cucumber and carrot	Serves 4 1 English cucumber, leave skin on and grate. If ordinary cucumbers are used, then peel.	Add 1 C freshly grated carrot.	Add 1 t crushed cumin.	Mix 1/2 t salt, freshly ground pepper. 1t sugar, 4t salad oil, 2t vinegar.	Toss salad well and serve in glass bowl.	Cucumbers are low in kilojoules Contains Minerals.
Cucumber and Onion	Serves 4 1 English cucumber grated.	Add 1 sliced onion	Chop 2 T coriander	Season with salt, pepper, lemon juice.	Served chilled.	Onions have Vit B_6, Vit C.
Carrot and pineapple	Serves 6 Grate 4 carrots	Add 1 C chopped pineapple	2 T crushed cumin 1 T chopped parsley	3 t sugar 1 t salt	Garnish with parsley	Carrots contain Carotene – Carrots are good for eyesight.

* South-African style barbecue.

Salad	Quantity and Preparations	Combined With	Herbs and Spices	Seasonings and Dressings	Presentation and Serving Suggestions	Nutrients Values and Tips
Sweet carrot salad	Serves 6 Clean and cut medium carrots into thin strips, Julienne style.	3 T golden syrup. 2 T salad oil	1/2 T crushed garlic, 1t chilli powder 3 cinnamon sticks.	2 T vinegar 1t salt	Place in glass bowl Garnish with a few sprigs of coriander herb. Sprinkle with chilli powder.	Same as above.
Corn and green pepper	Serves 4 2 x 410 g tins corn or 2 frozen corn.	Add 1/2 C green peppers chopped.	1/2 green chilli chopped 1/2 t mustard.	Stir well with 1/2 t salt 1 t olive oil.	Delicious when served over boiled potatoes.	Green or chilli peppers is said to give your mood a lift. Contains Capsaincin which causes a burning sensation in the mouth.
Green salad	Serves 6 A selection of different greens of lettuce, spinach, watercress.	Smother with 1/2 C yoghurt 2 T chopped chives	Spice with it crushed cumin 1/2 t crushed garlic.	A touch of salt.	Serve chilled.	There is a lot of fibre in green salad. Low in kilojoules Excellent for dieters.
Mushroom and pepper	Serves 4 300 g mushrooms sliced.	1 green pepper, quarter core and slice 1/4 c green onion chopped.	Rub over 1/2 t crushed garlic 2 T honey 2 T lemon juice	1 t salt 1/4 C salad oil.	A crunch mushroom salad. Serve with rice.	Mushrooms are low in kilojoules Contains Vit B_6.
Sweet melon	Serves 4 Dice 1 large ripe melon.	A sprinkle of sugar, a squeeze of lemon juice.	Chop 1 T mint	2 t chopped walnuts.	Present in deep glass bowl.	For Fibre, Contains Sugar.
Tomato salad	Serves 6 6 ripe tomatoes, slice 1cm thick		Chop 1 T thyme 1 sprig rosemary	Sprinkle over 1 t sugar, 2 t crushed cumin, and 1t salt.	Serve on large oval platter	Tomatoes are rich in Vit A and C.
Spinach salad	Serves 6 3 C young spinach leaves shredded.	1 onion sliced		1 t crushed garlic 1/2 C cream cheese 1 T milk, 1/2 t salt and 1/2 t pepper.	Place spinach on a platter and pour over cheese dressing.	Low in kilojoules. Contains Vit A, C, B6, Iron and Calcium.
Green peas and rice salad	Serves 4 1 C frozen peas steamed	2 C cooked rice 1 chopped tomato	Toss in 1/4 C chopped herbs of your choice	Pour 1 C salad cream or 1 C yoghurt, seasoned with 1 t salt 2 t cumin	Serve with steamed vegetables	Green peas contain Proteins, Vit B, C, Phosphorus and Iron. Rice is nutritious. Contains Vit B and minerals.

A mouthwatering North Indian feast with chana masala, raita and a large puri called bathura in the forefront. Home made cheese "paneer malai", chana dhodi and ladyfingers fry.

Vegetarian Main Course

Vegetables with herbs and spices
Mexican chilli con carne: spicy bean dish
Corn and cream bake
Macaroni brinjal bake
Easy baked beans casserole

Tomato soya mince
Khubi fry - cabbage supreme
Spicy coconut curry
Roasted brinjal curry
Bhaji fry - spinach fry
Pisang gorang - fried bananas
Sweet and sour spicy okra - lady fingers
Easy spicy tossed vegetables
Vegetables in yoghurt
Matar and baigan sakh - Green pea and brinjal curry
Gem squash bake
Mixed vegetable curry

Papdi ne vengan nu sakh - Indian beans with potatoes and brinjal
Fresh mealies tarkhari
Tarela patra - fried kachu delicacy
Mauritian vegetables in tomato gravy (rougaille)
Bhagereli baigan - stuffed baby brinjals
Greek moussaka

Vegetable bake
Gado Gado - Indonesian style with peanut sauce
Chana dhal ni moothia - lentil kebabs in tomato gravy
Stuffed Indian vegetables
Mango curry
Bhaji matar paneer - homemade cheese in smooth spinach and peas
Mushroom and cashewnut curry
Lemon and mushroom rice
Aromatic rice
Spicy rice

Vegetable biryani

Vegetables with herbs and spices

Vegetables	Preparation	Herbs, Spices, Seasonings	Serving Suggestions and Uses
Artichoke	Wash well, cut away stalk and cook in salted water for 25 minutes.	Smother in butter, chopped parsley	Serve warm. Also serve cold with a salad cream.
Asparagus	Wash, remove 3 cm from base of stalks, tie in bundle and stand in a saucepan of salted water. Cook for 25 minutes.	Serve with a touch of freshly ground black pepper.	Serve warm or serve cool as a salad and snack. Chop into sandwich filling with cheese. Delicious for quiches and pies.
Beans (green and French)	Snip and cut beans. Wash and stem young beans and drain.	Season with salt, pepper, butter and chopped lemon, thyme.	Serve warm or cool as salad. Serve with sauté almonds for a difference.
Brinjal (Eggplant or Aubergine)	Wash, pat dry. Slice lengthwise. Sprinkle with salt. Dab dry after a few minutes. Brush with butter and grill for 10 minutes.	Sprinkle cayenne, pepper and chopped coriander herb.	Serve as side dish or cover with yoghurt as a salad. Brinjals are excellent in casseroles. Use to thicken vegetable tarkharis.
Broccoli	Wash very well. Boil in salted water for 10 minutes.	Smother with butter, black pepper and chopped basil.	Serve also with sour cream or yoghurt, chopped nut and black pepper.
Brussel sprouts	Wash, trim stem and remove outer leaves. Boil in salted water for 12 minutes.	Toss in melted butter with a good pinch of nutmeg.	Serve as salad.
Butternut	Peel and cube. Steam for 15 minutes.	Mash into pulp. Season with salt, pepper, sugar or honey, nutmeg and butter.	Use to thicken soups and Indian dishes.
Cabbage	Slice thinly, wash well and drain. Boil for a few minutes.	Add chopped fresh chives. Season with freshly grated nutmeg, salt and pepper.	Stir fry with a little garlic. Use as a cold salad.
Carrots	Peel and cut into rings, match sticks or leave whole. Boil in salted water until tender.	Season with salt, sugar, butter and chopped parsley. Stir in a little cream and ground cinnamon for a change.	Use grated, cooked or stewed carrots for puddings, cakes, salads and soups. Glace carrots with a little honey in a saucepan and sprinkle with nuts.
Cauliflower	Cut into florets or leave whole. Boil in salted water.	Spice up with pepper cover cheese and chopped herbs and grill.	Stir fry cauliflower. Makes excellent soup. Bake with white sauce and cheese topping.
Celery	Keep fresh in fridge by leaving in water. Remove leaves, cut stalks and cook in salted water.	Saute in butter with a few mushrooms. Season with salt and pepper.	Celery is good for soup. Use leaves and stalks.
Courgettes (Baby marrow or zucchini)	Leave whole, scrub well and boil in salted water.	Toss in butter with nutmeg and freshly chopped fennel.	Courgettes can be stuffed, baked, pickled or eaten as a salad.

Vegetables	Preparation	Herbs, Spices, Seasonings	Serving Suggestions and Uses
Gem squash	Cut in half and boil in salted water. Also cook, whole, but pierce with a skewer.	Scoop out seeds and top with butter, pepper, a touch of sugar.	Fill a spoonful of steamed mix vegetables or green peas into squash. Also delicious if filled with cream style corn, topped with cheese and grilled.
Marrow	Peel and parboil in salted water.	Glace marrow by tossing in butter. Add a little honey and brown. Season with grated nutmeg.	Place cubes of parboiled marrow in oven proof dish. Cover with white sauce, bread crumbs, cheese and grill till brown.
Mushroom	Wash and peel mushroom cut in quarters or slice.	Sauté in butter with freshly crushed garlic, salt and black pepper.	Sauté 1 onion in butter. Toss in mushroom and season with garlic and salt. Use in soup, salad, sandwich fillings, quiches and casseroles.
Onions	Wash small onions and boil in salted water.	Sauté in butter, chopped parsley and black pepper.	Combine with slices of boiled potato. Season with salt and pepper. Cover with white sauce, top with herbs, cheddar cheese and grill. Also eat raw as a salad.
Peas	Shell fresh peas and cook in salted boiling water for 20 minutes till soft.	Toss peas in butter. Add 2 T milk, chopped mint, a pinch of sugar and salt.	Basil, oregano and tomato puree can also season peas to perfection.
Potatoes	Boil in salted water with a pinch of turmeric.	Fry in oil + ghee till golden brown.	Excellent with all meals. Rich in Vit C.

Two superb Italian dishes- corn & cream bake and macaroni brinjal bake.

MEXICAN CHILLI *CON CARNE* – SPICY BEAN DISH

| Serves 6 | Time : 60 mins |

200 g chilli soya mince
1 chopped onion
2 sticks of celery, sliced
1 green pepper, sliced
30 ml (2 T) sunflower oil
225 g tin chilli beans or baked beans
410 g tin tomatoes, chopped
750 ml (3 c) water
30 ml (2 T) cream

Heat the oil in a saucepan and fry the onion, celery and green pepper.

Stir in the beans and tomatoes.

Add the water and the soya mince and cook for about 10 minutes.

Add the cream immediately before the dish is to be served.

This is eaten with rice.

CORN AND CREAM BAKE

| Serves 4-6 | Time : 1 hr |

500 ml (2 c) whole kernels (tinned or frozen)
125 ml (1/2 c) fresh cream
2 small onions
2 large potatoes
1-2 chopped green chillies
125 ml (1/2 c) grated cheese

Chop the onions.

Boil the potatoes and cut into small cubes.

Mix the corn, cream, onions, potatoes and green chillies together.

Season with salt and freshly ground pepper.

Place the mixture into a shallow casserole dish.

Sprinkle the cheese evenly over the mixture.

Bake for 30 minutes at 180°C.

MACARONI BRINJAL BAKE

Serves 6 — Time : 30 mins

250 g macaroni
1 large brinjal, diced
500 ml (2 c) peeled, chopped tomatoes
2 onions, chopped
2 cloves of garlic
2-3 green chillies, finely chopped
Salt
Pepper
Oil or ghee (or half and half)
1/4 c grated cheese

Cook macaroni according to directions. When macaroni is cooked, drain and place aside.

Heat 4 T oil or ghee and fry the diced brinjal until the pieces turn brown. Remove the brinjal from the pan and place aside.

Sauté the onions and the garlic in the same oil. Add the tomatoes, chillies, salt and pepper and simmer for 15 to 20 minutes.

Remove from heat and mix the macaroni and brinjal into the tomato mixture.

Place into a baking dish and sprinkle the top with cheese.

Arrange 2 pieces of fried brinjal on top.

Bake for about 30 minutes in a moderate oven.

EASY BAKED BEANS CASSEROLE

Serves 2-4 — Time : 45 mins

410 g tin baked beans
1 onion, chopped
1 tomato, grated
Oil
Curry leaves
1 chopped pepper
4 green chillies (Optional)
Fenugreek seeds
Mustard seeds

1/2 t salt
1/2 t turmeric
1 t masala
1 dessert spoon vinegar
2 t sugar
Chopped fresh coriander leaves
3 potatoes, boiled
1 onion, sliced into rings
1 tomato, sliced into rings
1/2 c cheese

Heat oil.

Add the curry leaves, pepper, chillies, fenugreek and mustard seeds.

Fry in the oil for a short while.

Add chopped onion and braise.

Add the grated tomato and salt.

Place the turmeric and masala into the mixture and mix well.

Add the baked beans, vinegar and sugar. Mix well and add chopped fresh coriander leaves.

Mash the boiled potatoes with a little milk and salt and pepper to taste.

In a casserole dish place the baked bean mixture at the bottom of the dish and place the potato in a layer on top of the baked beans.

Place the sliced tomato and onion in the same way on top of the potato and place the grated cheese over the top of the layer of tomato and onion.

Bake for 15 minutes at 180°C.

Grill for a few minutes until the cheese is slightly brown.

TOMATO SAUCE/CHUTNEY

Serves 4 — Time: 15 mins

2 onions, chopped finely
3 tomatoes, chopped
30 ml (2 T) salad oil
Salt to taste
5 ml (1 T) sugar
1 green chilli (Optional)

Heat oil and saute onions until soft and golden.

Add tomatoes and seasonings.

Cover saucepan and cook for 20 minutes.

KHUBI FRY – CABBAGE SUPREME

Serves 4 — Time: 15 mins

500 g (1/2 medium) cabbage, sliced thinly
4 potatoes, cut into very thin chips
3 onions, sliced
125 ml (1/2 c) dhunia/coriander leaves, chopped
5 ml (1 t) green masala
7 ml (1 t) salt
15 ml (3 t) dhunia + jeera / coriander + cumin powder
2 ml (1/2 t) turmeric
10 ml (2 t) sugar
62 ml (1/4 c) cooking oil
5 ml (1 t) jeera/cumin seeds
5 ml (1 t) fenugreek seeds

Toss cabbage and vegetable in a large dish with the spices mixing well.

Heat the oil in a large saucepan with a well fitting lid.

Add mustard, cumin and fenugreek, then the cabbage mixture.

Keep the heat high for the first 5 minutes.

Keeping the lid on, turn the heat to low.

Simmer for 20 minutes.

Share my very special cabbage dish. I love serving this with puri (Indian bread) or rice.

TOMATO SOYA MINCE

Serves 4 — Time: 30 mins

1 quantity of tomato chutney*
125 g soya mince
5 ml (1 t) chopped chillies

Add the soya mince to the tomato chutney.

Add the chopped chillies.

Mix together well and heat through.

* See recipe of tomato chutney opposite.

SPICY COCONUT CURRY

Serves 4 — Time: 15 mins

2 chopped onions
10 ml (2 t) garlic, crushed
2 green chillies
60 ml (4 T) dessicated or grated coconut
1 piece of ginger 3 cm long
60 ml (4 T) fresh coriander leaves, chopped
5 ml (1 t) cumin seeds
5 ml (1 t) turmeric powder
15 ml (3 t) poppy seeds
8 curry leaves
30 ml (2 T) ghee
Salt
500 ml coconut milk or creamed coconut
15 ml (3 t) lemon juice

Mince the onions with the garlic, chillies, coconut, ginger, coriander, cumin seeds, turmeric powder and the poppy seeds.

This should make a paste.

Place ghee in a pan and heat.

Add curry leaves and paste.

Cook paste in the ghee for 5 minutes.

Combine salt and coconut milk with paste and simmer for 10 minutes.

Mix in the lemon juice.

Serve with rice.

A South Indian gravy which is served over a bowl of piping hot rice.

A traditional dish of roasted brinjal curry.

ROASTED BRINJAL CURRY

Serves 4   Time : 45 mins

2 large brinjals (washed and dried)
2 medium onions, chopped
45 ml (3 T) oil
5 ml (1 t) fresh ginger, chopped finely
3 large chopped tomatoes
2 green chillies, chopped
5 ml (1 t) red chilli powder
250 ml (1 c) frozen green peas
30 ml (2 T) freshly grated coconut (dessicated coconut may be used)
Salt to taste
1 bunch fresh coriander

Smear some oil on skin of the brinjal.

Grill in oven until it is evenly brown on both sides. If done on a hot plate or open fire turn the brinjal occasionally while roasting.

Peel and chop the brinjals when cool.

Heat the oil in a pan and cook the onions until they are golden brown.

Add ginger and stir.

Add the tomatoes and cook until the oil starts to separate from the mixture.

Add green chillies, red chilli powder, coconut, salt and brinjals.

Add the peas and continue cooking until the peas are tender.

Garnish with coriander leaves.

A delicious brinjal delicacy. Roasted or grilled brinjal cooks into an aromatic delight.

BHAJI FRY – SPINACH FRY

Serves 4   Time : 25 mins

500 g spinach (1 bunch)
45 ml (3 T) cooking oil
5 ml (1 t) jeera/cumin seeds
2 onions, sliced
2 ml (1/2 t) fresh garlic, pounded
2 ml (1/2 t) red chilli powder
2 ml (1/2 t) salt
1 ml (1/4 t) turmeric

Cut thick veins from spinach leaves.

Soak in cold water for 5 minutes, the sand and soil will settle out.

Rinse spinach several times, then chop finely.

Heat oil in a pan and add cumin seeds.

Brown for a few seconds then add sliced onions and garlic.

Fry onions until brown and soft.

Add spinach, chilli powder, salt and turmeric.

Leave the pan uncovered and cook on medium heat.

Let all the moisture from the spinach evaporate.

Stir and serve when the spinach and onion have softened.

An excellent accompaniment with lentil rice.

PISANG GORANG – FRIED BANANAS

| Serves 2-4 | Time : 10-15 mins |

4 bananas
Butter

Peel the bananas.

Fry gently in butter until the bananas are golden brown.

Serve the bananas warm.

Serve with brown rice and rice flour wafers.

SWEET AND SOUR SPICY *OKRA* (LADY FINGERS)

| Serves 4 | Time : 40 mins |

500 g okra/ lady fingers
60 ml (1/4 c) cooking oil
5 ml (1 t) jeera/cumin seeds
1 onion, chopped
5 ml (1 t) fresh garlic, pounded
5 ml (1 t) fresh ginger, pounded
2 ml (1/2 t) salt
2 ml (1/2 t) sugar
2 ml (1/2 t) red or green masala
1 tomato, chopped
15 ml (1 T) lemon juice
30 ml (2 T) dhunia/coriander leaves, chopped

Rinse okra well and cut into 25 mm pieces.

Heat the oil in a saucepan and add cumin seeds to brown for 10 seconds.

Add the onions and fry till soft (about 3 minutes).

Add the okra and the remaining ingredients and cover saucepan.

Lower the heat and cook gently for 30 minutes until all the moisture evaporates.

Serve immediately.

EASY SPICY TOSSED VEGETABLES

| Serves 4 | Time : 20 mins |

2 medium carrots, cut thinly into strips
250 ml (1 c) green beans, sliced thinly
1 large onion, sliced
250 ml (1 c) green peas, frozen
1 medium green pepper, sliced
30 ml (2 T) melted margarine or butter
5 ml (1 t) ginger, crushed
5ml (1 t) black pepper, freshly ground
Salt to taste

Using a heavy saucepan, fry onion in oil until soft.

Add ginger.

Toss for a few seconds.

Add vegetables, season with salt and pepper and toss at fairly high heat for a few minutes.

Cover saucep
an and cook on low heat until vegetables are done.

A superb dish for vegetarians, especially if served with mashed potato and aromatic rice.

VEGETABLES IN YOGHURT

Serves 6　　Time : 35 mins

100 g fresh green beans, sliced
2 drumsticks (Indian vegetable) cut into pieces
2 medium carrots cubed – 1 large brinjal cut into lengths
50 g cubed pumpkin or dhodi (Indian marrow)
1 green pepper, sliced
1 gem squash or choux choux, peeled and cubed
2 green bananas, sliced thickly
5 ml (1 t) salt
10 strands of saffron
4 green chillies
250 ml (1 c) fresh coconut, grated
10 ml (2 t) cumin seeds
250 ml (1 c) cream/yoghurt
30 ml (2 T) oil
5 ml (1 t) mustard seeds
10 (1 t) curry leaves
5 ml (1 t) chilli powder
1 t sugar

Pre cook the vegetables in a little water with saffron and salt until soft.
Remove from heat.
Liquidise or pound cumin seeds, green chillies and coconut with a little water to make a paste.
Add paste to vegetables and stir cream/yoghurt into vegetable pot, add sugar.
Cook the mixture for a few minutes at low heat while stirring constantly.
Separately heat oil in a small pot.
Add mustard seeds and curry leaves.
When the mustard seeds splutter combine this with the vegetables.
Simmer gently for a few minutes.
Serve with basmati rice.

This splendid combination of vegetables offer superbly gentle flavours. Saffron delights in colouring this dish. Serve with fragrant basmati rice or long grain white rice and a raita (fresh relish)

Variations – Roasted Vegetables
Use the same ingredients. Mix all together. Leave out the cream or yoghurt. Heat 1/2 c ghee in a large saucepan. Place all vegetables and fry for 10 mins till well coated with ghee. Cover sauce pan and gently cook for 40 mins until soft.

MATAR AND BAIGAN SAKH – GREEN PEA AND BRINJAL CURRY

Serves 6　　Time : 30 mins

200 g green beans, fresh, cut into 25 mm strips, optional
200 g peas, frozen may also be used
200 g brinjals, wash and cut into 25 mm cubes
100 g onions, chopped
5 ml (1 t) turmeric
7 ml (1 1/2 t) salt
50 mm piece of ginger, crushed to a paste
5 ml (1 t) red chilli powder
10 ml (2 t) coriander seeds, crushed
10 ml (2 t) cumin seeds, crushed
30 ml (2 T) oil
2 (75 mm) pieces of cinnamon sticks
5 ml (1 t) tymol (cumin can be used instead of tymol)
100 g fresh ripe tomatoes, chopped
30 ml (2 T) coriander leaves, chopped

Mix beans, peas, brinjals, onions, turmeric, salt, ginger, chilli powder, coriander and cumin powder well together in a bowl.
Heat oil in a saucepan.
Place in cinnamon sticks and tymol (or cumin) and brown for a few seconds.
Add the spiced vegetables to the pot, stir and cover the saucepan.
Simmer on a low heat for 20 minutes.
Add tomatoes and cover; cook for 10 minutes.
Garnish with coriander.
Serve with warm chapattis and pickles. Ideal to fill up a roll and take along to work or to school as lunch.

The Bengalore vegetable market boasts the finest brinjals. Gleaming and attractive, they make tasty dishes.

"Saag" - a beautiful mixture of vegetables cooked with broad beans usually served with steamed rice.

GEM SQUASH BAKE

| Serves 6 | Time : 15 mins |

6 gem squash (1,5 kg)
60 ml (30 g) flour
2 ml (1/2 t) garlic
30 ml (15 g) butter
500 ml (2 c) milk
2 ml (1/2 t) salt
2 ml (1/2 t) pepper
125 ml (1/2 c) cheese, grated
250 ml (1 c) bread crumbs

Boil the gem squash.

Mix the flour, butter and garlic together to form a paste.

Place into a saucepan.

When the butter is melted and the flour has been braised, add the milk gradually, stirring constantly to prevent lumps.

Stir constantly until the sauce thickens.

Season with the salt and pepper and add half the cheese.

Mix well.

Combine the other cheese with the bread crumbs.

Halve and de-seed the boiled gem squashes.

Scoop the flesh out of the halves and place into a shallow baking dish.

Smooth out the pulp and pour the cheese sauce over the top covering the gem squash.

Sprinkle the bread crumb mixture over the cheese sauce and place under the grill for about 10 minutes until the top is browned.

Variations

Choux choux, pumpkin or any squash may be used.

MIXED VEGETABLE CURRY

| Serves 2-4 | Time : 10-15 mins |

1 C (250 ml) green beans – sliced
2 med pieces butternut
1 large potato
1/2 small brinjal

60 ml (4 T) ghee
15 ml (1 T) crushed aniseed
1 large chilli sliced lengthwise
5ml (1 t) ginger masala (fresh root ginger crushed to a fine paste)
5ml (1 t) chilli powder
250 ml (1 cup) buttermilk
Salt
Pinch Sugar
15 ml (1 T) chana flour
125 ml (1/2 c) cream (Optional)
Coconut (Optional)

Cube the vegetables.

In a bowl mix buttermilk with chana flour to make a smooth paste. Add cream with chilli powder, salt and sugar.

Heat ghee in a saucepan. Add aniseed, sliced chilli and ginger. Allow to brown.

Add buttermilk mixture and stir until gravy thickens.

Season vegetables with salt and turmeric and toss into gravy. Garnish with coconut. Add 2/3 c water. Cover and cook on a low heat.

Serve with piping hot rice or Indian bread.

PAPADI NE VENGAN NU SAKH – INDIAN BEANS WITH POTATOES AND BRINJALS

Serves 4-6   Time : 30-40 mins

500 g green beans, cut in 40 mm pieces
60 ml (4 T) cooking oil
2 sticks cinnamon, 3 cm each
5 ml (1 t) cumin seeds
5 ml (1 t) crushed ginger
1 small onion, chopped
2 ml (1/2 t) salt
5 ml (1 t) turmeric
2 ml (1/2 t) red chilli powder
2 potatoes cut in 40 mm cubes
100 g brinjals, skinned and cut in 25 mm cubes
5 ml (1 t) coriander – cumin powder
1 tomato, chopped finely
15 ml (1 T) coriander leaves, chopped

Wash green beans and place in colander.

Heat the oil in a saucepan and add the cumin seeds and cinnamon sticks, ginger and onions, and allow to fry for 2 to 3 minutes until the onions are translucent.

Add the vegetables and the remaining ingredients, leaving the coriander leaves and tomato aside.

Cover saucepan and cook over low heat for 20 minutes.

Add the tomato and coriander leaves.

Stir and cook for 10 more minutes.

Water should not be added to Indian vegetables when cooking.

A side dish which may also be used for any fresh Indian beans such as gwarferi, toover ni sing, papadi or toover sing. Green beans are always available fresh or frozen, and will make a substantial meal served with warm roti or hot toast and pickles.

I use the spicy beans cold for a sandwich or snackwich filler. Try as a topping combined with crunchy sliced onions and cheese on a slice of whole wheat bread (place under griller for a few minutes). As a variation, add 100 g green peas.

FRESH MEALIES TARKHARI

Serves 4   Time : 60 mins

500 g sweetcorn, freshly cut off the cob
1 c milk
1 c water
30 ml (2 T) cream, optional
30 ml (2 T) melted ghee
2 ml (1/2 t) garlic
5 ml (1 t) ginger
5 ml (1 t) salt
5 ml (1 t) sugar
2 ml (1/2 t) turmeric
5 ml (1 t) green masala
Coriander leaves or parsley for garnish

Heat the ghee and braise the ginger and garlic.

Add the turmeric, salt, green masala.

Then add the mealies.

Add the water and the rest of the ingredients.

Cover with a lid and allow to cook on a low heat.

Stir frequently so that the mealies remain separate.

Garnish with fresh coriander herbs or parsley.

TARELA PATRA – FRIED *KACHU* * LEAVES DELICACY

Serves 6 — Time : 60 mins

24 patra or kachu leaves or 20 spinach leaves
250 ml (1 c) chana flour or besan flour
175 ml (3/4 c) bread flour
175 ml (3/4 c) maize flour or 375 ml (1 1/2 c) plain flour
10 ml (2 t) salt
2 ml (1/2 t) bicarbonate of soda
5 ml (1 t) green masala
5 ml (1 t) red masala
2 ml (1/2 t) ginger
2 ml (1/2 t) garlic
5 ml (1 t) turmeric
10 ml (2 t) dhunia/jeero (coriander/cumin) powder
10 ml (2 t) gharam masala
22 ml (1 1/2 T) melted ghee
15 ml (3 t) sugar
5 ml (1 t) tymol
250 ml (1 c) buttermilk or sour milk
Water to make a soft dropping consistency
Oil for frying

Mix the flour, ghee, sugar and spices, then add buttermilk and water.

Make a soft batter (not as thin as pancake batter).

Wash the leaves and cut off the stems and remove any thick veins in the leaves so that the leaves may be flattened.

Roll with a rolling pin to flatten.

Using the hands, coat each leaf with the batter, then fold the outer edges towards the middle, then fold up from the bottom so that you get a rectangle about 60 mm x 30 mm.

Shallow fry each rectangle in oil in a frying pan for about 5 minutes on each side (the leaves should be golden brown and starting to crispen).

To complete the cooking, place the fried rectangles in a steamer and stem for 5 to 10 minutes until the leaves are cooked.

* From the luscious vegetation of the island of Mauritius, kachu leaves grow in great abundance. A superb recipe to try, especially for Indian cooks. This authentic recipe will lend a classical flavour to a leaf which can be taken for granted because of its generous growth. Try this superb vegetarian gourmet creation. <u>Kachu</u> (India), <u>taro</u> or <u>eddoe leaf</u> (English), <u>colocasia esclenta</u> (scientific), <u>brède songe</u> (creole).

STEAMED *PATRA* LEAVES – *Variation*

Serves 6 — Time : 60 mins

Make the batter as above.

Spread 15 ml (1 T) over one leaf.

Place another leaf over the battered leaf.

Spread the top again with 15 ml (1 T) of batter.

Repeat in this manner until 6 leaves have been placed on top each other.

Fold the two side edges over and press flat.

Roll the pile up into a long swiss roll shape.

Repeat with remaining leaves.

Place rolls into a steam cooker and cook by this method for 45 to 60 minutes.

Remove rolls from steamer and cool.

These rolls can be frozen at this stage until needed.

Slice into 12 mm rounds.

Heat 250 ml (1 c) oil in a frying pan and fry slices for 2 minutes on either side until crispy.

Serve hot with wedges of lemon and coriander or mint chutney.

Serve as starters or with cocktails.

May be served with chutney, the deep fried Indian breads. Place on a fried puri for puri patta.

Puri patta are internationally known.

Cauliflower, vegetables and chips served on a golden Mauritian beach, all smothered with a "rougaille" sauce.

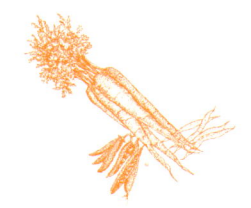

MAURITIAN VEGETABLES WITH TOMATO GRAVY – *Rougaille*

| Serves 6 | Time : 60 mins |

1 large cauliflower
20 french beans
10 baby carrots
6 potatoes for thin chips
Oil for deep frying potatoes

Tomato Gravy (Rougaille)
2 onions
3 cup chopped tomatoes
2 green chillies
1 tsp garlic, chopped
1/4 cup oil
Salt to taste

Remove outer green leaves of cauliflower.

Trim neatly leaving the head whole. Wash thoroughly under running water.

Snip the ends of the beans and wash.

Scrape carrots and rinse.

Place vegetables in a large saucepan and boil in 2 cup of salted water for 15 mins or until cooked but firm.

Meanwhile, make a tomato gravy by frying chopped onion in oil until golden brown.

Add tomatoes with chilli, garlic and salt to taste. A pinch of sugar may be added.

Cook for 15 mins on a medium heat until tomato gravy is done. Keep warm.

Cut peeled potatoes into thin chips. Dry well in cloth and deep fry in oil until crisp and cooked. Leave aside.

To assemble, present the warm cauliflower on a large platter, taking care not to break the whole head.

Arrange the drained vegetables around.

Pour tomato gravy over the top and decorate with potato chips.

A delicious party dish to serve with rice and salads.

BHAGERELI BAIGAN – STUFFED BABY BRINJALS

| Serves 4 | Time : 40 mins |

500 g baby brinjals
100 g peanuts, coarsely chopped
2 T sesame seeds
250 g green peas, fresh or frozen
2 T coriander leaves, chopped
4 T freshly grated coconut or 3 T dessicated coconut
1 1/2 t sugar
1 1/2 t dhunia /jeero powder (coriander/cumin)
1/2 t fresh ginger
1 t crushed soomph (large aniseed)
1/2 t green masala or 1 chopped green chilli
1/2 t salt
1/4 cup cooking oil
1/4 t hing / asafoetida powder

Wash baby brinjals and pat dry with a towel.

Slit lengthwise twice, but only three quarters of the way down the brinjals. Season with a pinch of salt.

Chop peas coarsely in a food processor or mincer. Put in a bowl with coriander leaves, coconut, sugar, dhunia/jeero, ginger, green masala and 1/2 t salt, peanuts and sesame seeds.

Mix this stuffing well and insert a good quantity in each brinjal, using up all the mixture.

Heat the oil in a saucepan, sprinkle in the asafoetida and brown for 10 seconds.

Gently arrange brinjals and excess stuffing in the same saucepan and fry for about 3 minutes over medium heat. Turn brinjals over and cover saucepan.

Simmer for another 20 minutes.

Baby brinjals (baby aubergines) have delicate sweet flavour, with a subtle bitterness found in the skins, where the vitamins lie. Serve the stuffed brinjal with roti, papadums and a pickle. There is an art to stuffing vegetables with the correct spices and ingredients. Here the coconut gives a characteristic flavour.

VARIATIONS

Instead of Brinjals substitute one of the following vegetables.

Stuffed Bhindi – Lady Fingers
Wash lady fingers and pat dry. Cut lengthwise keeping base intact. Following same method.

Stuffed Okra – Bitter Gourd
Wash okra and pat dry. Cut as above and remove seeds. Stuff and follow same method.

Stuffed Tomatoes
Use same method as basic recipe.

GREEK MOUSSAKA

| Serves 6 | Time : 1 hr 30 mins |

600 g brinjals
250 ml (1 c) brown lentils
500 ml (2 c) water
Salt
25 ml (5 t) olive oil or vegetable oil
1 seeded and diced green pepper
1 large onion, chopped
2 cloves of garlic, crushed
300 g cleaned and sliced mushrooms
400 g peeled and diced tomatoes
2 ml (1/2 t) cinnamon, ground
10 ml parsley, chopped
2 ml (1/2 t) salt
10 ml (2 t) brown sugar
1 bay leaf
1 chopped green chilli
30 ml (2 T) butter, melted
60 ml (1/4 c) flour
500 ml (2 c) warmed milk
60 g feta cheese, grated
45 g parmesan cheese
Pepper

Slice the brinjal into 5 mm slices.

Heat the oil and fry the brinjals until both sides are soft and golden brown.

Sort through the lentils and clean them.

Once the lentils are rinsed, boil them in the salted water until the water is absorbed and the lentils are soft.

Sauté the onion, garlic and green pepper in heated olive oil.

Place the mushrooms into the pan and fry until softened. Then add the sugar, cinnamon, salt, parsley, tomatoes and the bay leaf and green chilli.

Cook gently for 20 minutes in a covered pan.

Stir the mixture every so often.

Take out the bay leaf and add mixture to the lentils.

To make the cheese sauce, melt the butter, add the flour and braise for a few moments. Add the warmed milk slowly, stirring constantly. Continue stirring the sauce until it becomes thick. Add the feta cheese and stir well.

When assembling the moussaka, place a layer of brinjal at the base of a baking dish, using half of the brinjals.

Place the lentil mixture over the slices.

Place another layer of brinjals on top of the lentils and cover with the cheese sauce.

Sprinkle the parmesan cheese over the top of the sauce.

Bake at 180°C for 45 to 60 minutes.

VEGETABLE BAKE

| Serves 6 | Time : 1 hr |

500 g mixed vegetables cut in small pieces (frozen may be used)
1/2 c chopped fenugreek leaves or 1 c chopped spinach
1 small chopped onion
2 T green masala or green chilli, chopped
1 T dhunia/jeero (coriander/cumin) powder
1 t turmeric
2 t salt
3/4 cup cake flour
3/4 cup semolina or crushed wheat
1/2 cup milk
2 T chana flour
1/3 cup cooking oil
1/3 cup ghee
1 t gharam masala
1 t sugar

Garnish

4 T sesame seeds
2 T coriander leaves, chopped
3 t chilli powder

Place all the ingredients in a bowl and mix well.

Spread mixture out in a casserole dish and sprinkle with sesame seeds, coriander leaves and chilli powder.

Bake in moderate oven (160 °C) for 45 minutes.

GADO GADO WITH PEANUT SAUCE
Indonesian Style

Serves 4 — Time : 45 mins

250 ml (1 c) peanut butter
60 ml (4 T) water
5 ml (1 t) lemon juice
500 g vegetables of your choice, e.g. green beans, cauliflower, carrots, mushrooms.

Cut vegetables into small portions and boil in salted water until cooked

Leave aside in a casserole.

Heat peanut butter in a small saucepan.

Add water and lemon juice to form a liquid.

Cook on low heat stirring constantly for 10 minutes.

Pour over vegetables and serve warm with brown rice.

CHANA DHAL NI MOOTHIA – LENTIL KEBABS IN TOMATO GRAVY

Serves 6 — Time : 70 mins

500 ml (2 c) chana dhal (split chickpeas)
250 ml (1 c) oil for frying
4 ml (3/4 t) salt, or to taste
A pinch of turmeric
5 ml (1 t) red masala
2 ml (1/2 t) ginger, crushed
5 ml (1 t) garlic, crushed
5 ml (1 t) crushed cumin
10 ml (2 t) crushed coriander seeds

For gravy

2 onions
4 tomatoes
2 potatoes, peeled and diced
4 cinnamon sticks
6 cloves
125 ml (1/2 c) chopped coriander leaves
2 ml (1/2 t) salt
2 ml (1/2 t) turmeric
5 ml (1 t) sugar
180 ml (1/3 c) oil
Garnish (1 t) ghurum masala

Soak washed lentils overnight in water.

Drain well the next day and put a grinder or food processor to make a fine mixture.

Add spices of the lentil kebabs, i.e. salt, turmeric, red masala, ginger, garlic, cumin, coriander.

Place a little mixture into the palm of your hand and make little balls.

Heat oil in a wok or deep pot and gently fry balls until golden in colour.

Fry all the balls and leave aside.

To make gravy heat 180 ml oil in a saucepan.

Add masalas, fry gently, then add onions and allow to brown.

Add tomatoes and potatoes.

Cover saucepan.

Cook for 10 minutes.

Now add lentil balls.

Add chopped coriander and a little water to make a gravy.

Cover and cook for 15 minutes.

Garnish with more coriander and ghurum masala.

Serve with lemon wedges and roti.

A platter of delicately stuffed vegetables.
Forefront: left- large chilli, right lady finger(okra).
Above- okra, brinjal and tomato.

STUFFED INDIAN VEGETABLES

| Serves 4 | Time : 1hr 10 mins |

500 g of any of the vegetables mentioned below
200 g of fresh green peas coarsely grinded in mincer
1/4 c chana dhal
1/4 c urad dhal
4 t grated fresh coconut (dried coconut can be used)
4 red chillies
2 fresh green chillies
2 t crushed cumin seeds
4 t crushed coriander seeds
1 t salt
1/4 t t hing/ asafoetida powder
2 t lemon juice
1 t sugar

Place dhal into a pan and heat to roast (a dry roast).

Grind the dhal to a paste using lemon juice, chillies, coconut, seeds, salt, hing and sugar. Add water if necessary. Make a good mixture.

Now add the 200 g of peas and mix again.

Prepare vegetables by washing and patting dry.

Cut brinjals lengthwise twice, but only three quarters of the way down the brinjal leaving the base intact.

Other vegetables could be cut similarly.

Stuff the vegetables with the mixture.

Heat the oil in a saucepan.

Carefully place stuffed vegetables side by side, not on top of each other cover and simmer gently for 15 mins.

Remove lid and turn vegetables over with two forks. Fry on both sides.

Serve hot with fresh roti and coconut chutney.

A new avenue to Vegetarian. Cooking can be experienced by developing the art of stuffing simple vegetables.

Long tropical brinjals, okra or lady fingers, bitter gourd, tomatoes, green peppers or even the humble squash can be enhanced with tantalizing and exciting stuffings. An excellent basic stuffing is one made with coarsely grinded vegetables and coconut.

MANGO CURRY

| Serves 6 | Time : 1 hr |

1 kg green mangoes, wash, peel and cut into quarters
125 ml (1/2 c) sugar
8 cloves garlic, slivered
3 red dry chillies
2,5 ml (1/2 t) turmeric
5 ml (1 t) salt
30 ml (2 T) oil
7,5 ml (1 1/2 t) jeera/ cumin seeds
7,5 ml (1 1/2 t) methi – fenugreek seeds
5 ml (1 t) mustard seeds
5 ml (1 t) freshly pounded green or red chilli
3 medium tomatoes, grated

Heat oil, add methi, cumin, mustard seeds, garlic and chillies.

Fry till garlic begins to change colour.

Add grated tomatoes, mango pieces, rest of spices and the sugar. Cover pot.

Allow to simmer slowly till sugar and spices are well blended with mangoes and tomatoes.

Alternative method:

Instead of grating tomatoes cut them in quarters or select small gem tomatoes and halve them.

Simmer curry slowly, open lid at frequent intervals and spoon the sugar and spices over the mangoes and tomatoes taking care that the latter do not get mashed up.

When serving arrange the tomato halves in between the mango pieces.

A delicious tropical treat.

Paneer- Homemade cheese is made for "Paneer Malai".
Cheese making is an art which requires a little time.

BHAJI MATAR PANEER – HOMEMADE CHEESE IN SMOOTH SPINACH AND PEAS

| Serves 4 plus 3 hours for cheese making | Time : 40 mins |

Paneer

1 l (4 c) milk
30 ml (2 T) lemon juice
30 ml (2 T) melted ghee or butter
30 ml (2 T) cooking oil
2 ml (1/2 T) rai/mustard seeds
2 onions, chopped
2 ml (1/2 t) salt
2 ml (1/2 t) fresh ginger, pounded
2 ml (1/2 t) red masala
200 g frozen spinach (fine texture) OR
1 bunch fresh spinach (simmer for 15 mins in
250 ml (1 c) hot water & purée)
250 ml (1 c) frozen peas

Garnish

15 ml (1 T) dhunia/coriander leaves, chopped

Paneer

Bring the milk to the boil in a saucepan. Allow to boil once, then add the lemon juice, removing saucepan from heat.

Stir until the whey separates.

Spread the muslin cloth in a colander and pour in mixture.

Tie the ends of the cloth to form a bag for the cheese.

Allow the whey to run off and let the bag stand for 2 hours. Then squeeze out excess liquid by pressing.

Cut the cheese into small cubes.

Fry cheese cubes gently in ghee for 1 minute and place aside.

Heat the oil in a saucepan and add mustard seeds. Allow to pop. Add onions and fry for 3 minutes. Add the remaining spices, spinach and peas.

Simmer for 20 minutes with the lid on.

Add the cheese cubes and simmer for another 3 minutes.

Garnish with the coriander leaves.

This delicate vegetarian dish is one of India's specialities, with the homemade paneer or cheese contributing a creamy texture and flavour. I serve paneer with hot roti. Paneer may be prepared with various vegetables, but the spinach and peas combination remains a favourite. You will need muslin or any clean, soft cloth to make the cheese.

MUSHROOM AND CASHEW NUT CURRY

| Serves 6 | Time : 35 mins |

500 g button mushrooms – cut into quarters
1 medium onion – chopped
2 tomatoes – chopped
3 T (45 ml) ghee or melted butter
100 g crushed cashew or almond nuts
1/2 t (2 ml) crushed garlic
1/2 t (2 ml) turmeric
1 fresh green chilli – chopped
A few saffron strands
Salt to taste
125 ml (1/2 c) yoghurt
1 T (5 ml) ghurum masala
2 T (30 ml) dhunia/coriander leaves – chopped

Heat ghee in pot. Add onions and allow to brown. Add nuts, garlic, turmeric and green chilli. Braise for a few seconds. Toss in mushrooms, tomatoes, salt and saffron strands.

Cover pot and simmer for 12 minutes.

Stir in yoghurt. Cook for further 5 minutes.

Garnish with ghurum masala and chopped dhunia leaves.

LEMON AND MUSHROOM RICE

| Serves 4 | ⌚ Time : 1 hr |

625 ml (3 c) long grain or basmati rice
60 ml (4 T) ghee or cooking oil
3 medium onions
Juice of 1 lemon – 3 T lemon juice (optional)
300 g mushrooms, washed and diced
10 ml (2 t) fresh garlic, pounded
7 ml (1 1/2 t) fresh ginger, pounded
5 ml (1 t) salt
10 ml (2 t) dhunia-jeero/coriander-cumin powder
750 ml (3 c) warm water

In large flat saucepan, heat the ghee or oil, add onions and garlic and fry for 7 minutes or until soft.

Add the lemon juice and mushrooms and sauté for two minutes.

Wash rice and add to saucepan with salt, ginger, coriander-cumin and warm water.

Stir well.

Cover and allow to cook for 45 minutes over low heat until rice has absorbed all the moisture.

Stir up with a fork and serve.

AROMATIC RICE

| Serves 6 | ⌚ Time : 45 mins |

625 ml (3 c) long grain or basmati rice
5 ml (1 t) salt

45 ml (3 T) ghee or cooking oil
5 elaichi/cardamom pods
5 lavang/cloves
3 tuj/cinnamon sticks, 4 cm each
2 large onions, chopped
125 ml (1/2 c) water

Cook rice with the salt, place in a colander and run cold water through it so that the excess starch may be rinsed away.

Then season with 2 ml (1/2 t) more salt if necessary.

Use a large flat saucepan with a lid.

Heat the ghee (use more if needed) and add cloves, cardamom and cinnamon.

Quickly add the onions and allow to brown over a medium heat for 3 to 5 minutes.

Add rice and mix with the onions.

Add 125 ml (1/2 c) water and cover pot.

Simmer on the lowest heat for 30 minutes or until rice has heated through and absorbed the aromas.

Feast of rice dishes- spicy rice, pulao, biryani, lemon rice and aromatic rice.

SPICY RICE

Serves 6 — Time : 45 mins

2 cups rice – large grain
4 T melted butter or margarine
6 cloves garlic, crushed
1 t crushed ginger
1/2 t saffron (soak in 1/4 cup hot water)
Juice of 1/2 lemon
1 1/2 large onions, sliced
4 T yoghurt
4 T milk
2 green chillies, sliced lengthwise
2 t salt
2 small potatoes, diced
1/2 cup frozen peas
1/2 cup diced carrots
1/2 cup frozen beans
1 cup chopped cabbage
2 hard boiled eggs for garnish
2 T chopped nuts – walnuts, cashew, almonds

Cook rice with 1 t salt until done.

Place in a colander and allow the excess water to drain.

Meanwhile heat margarine in saucepan and fry the sliced onions until soft and brown.

Remove half the onions and keep aside for decorating.

Add the chopped vegetables, ginger, garlic, chillies.

1 t salt and stir fry for 2 minutes.

Then toss in rice and mix well together.

Pour yoghurt, milk, lemon juice and saffron with water over the top of the rice.

Cover saucepan and allow to simmer for 30 minutes on a medium heat.

To serve arrange pilau on a large platter.

Top with fried onions, sliced boiled eggs and sprinkle with nuts.

VEGETABLE BIRYANI

Serves 6 — Time : 60 mins

750 g long grain white or basmati rice
1 kg frozen mixed vegetables
5 lavang/cloves
3 tuj/cinnamon sticks, 50 mm each
5 elaichi/cardamom pods
500 g (2 c) masoor/brown lentils
375 ml (1 1/2 c) ghee or oil
2 large onions, sliced
6 potatoes, halved
200 g cabbage, halved
200 g mushrooms, quartered (optional)
5 ml (1 t) turmeric
7 ml (1 1/2 t) salt
10 ml (2 t) green chillies, chopped finely
15 ml (1 T) sugar
5 ml (1 t) fresh ginger, pounded
5 ml (1 t) fresh garlic, pounded
2 chillies, sliced lengthwise
10 limri/curry leaves
375 ml (1 1/2 c) buttermilk
2 ml (1/2 t) kesar/saffron, soaked for 15 minutes in 125 ml (1/2 c) hot water
125 ml (1/2 c) dhunia/coriander leaves, chopped

Parboil rice in salted water with the cloves, cinnamon and cardamom.

Drain rice in colander and run through cold water to remove excess starch.

Wash lentils and cook in 500 ml (2 c) unsalted water for 30 minutes until soft.

Fry slices onions in 180 ml (3/4 c) ghee until golden brown in remaining ghee (add more if needed).

Place washed vegetables in a large bowl.

Add turmeric, salt, green chillies, curry leaves and half the coriander leaves.

Mix well.

Pour buttermilk over.

Using a large oven-proof dish or suitable pot, place 125 ml (1/2 c) ghee at the bottom (use frying ghee).

Mix rice with vegetables, onions and potatoes.

Place into a pot.

Pour saffron water and ghee over the top.

Sprinkle with the chopped coriander leaves.

Bake in a preheated oven at 180°C for 1 hour or on top of stove plate for 45 mins on a low heat.

Pulses

Vaal ni dhakoo - thick bean soup
Palak dhal - Spinach dhal
Kabuli chana - whole chick pea
Creamed lentils
Sprouted moong - sprouted green lentils
Toovar sekta ni sing - lentil dhal with drumsticks
Masoor ni dhal - Spinach red lentil curry

Moong - green lentils
Dhal-e-dhodi -- split chickpea dhal

A selection of pulses.

Split Chickpea/Chana Dhal

This lentil is second only to wheat in nutritive value. In its whole form it is known as the chickpea. Chana is the split form, resembling yellow corn in shape and colour. It also resembles the yellowish split pea sold in supermarkets.

Chana is also known as Bengal gram. Chana dhal is ground into chana flour, the only flour used for traditional Indian savouries like chilli bites or the deep fried noodles called 'sev'.

Chana dhal acts as a general tonic when it is steeped overnight in water and chewed in the morning with a helping of honey.

Whole Chickpea/whole chana

This large heart shaped beige pea is India's favourite snack food, whether spiced, boiled, grilled or crushed. With its high nutritive value, chana cannot be dismissed as junk food.

Kabuli chana is a variety that is made into a delicious dish garnished with onion rings and served with large puri or fried breads.

Dried Indian Beans/Chori Beans

These dark brown beans are round and flat with a spot on one side. They provide a sumptuous main dish for vegetarians.

Black Eyes Beans/Lombhia Beans

These beige oval shaped beans with the dark dot on their side have a slightly smoky flavour and are prepared in the same manner as whole moong.

Brown Lentils/Masoor Dhal

These round flat lentils are used specifically for biryanis or rice dishes, and may be made into a soup. Their earthy flavour can be dull unless well spiced.

Pink Split/Masoor Ni Dhal

These round, flat salmon coloured lentils are actually brown lentils in split form, with the outer husks removed.

Quick cooking, with a pleasant mild taste, they easily absorb the flavour of curry leaves, whole green chillies and garlic.

A delicious soup may be prepared from them in a very short time.

Yellow Split Moong Lentils/Moong Dhal

These small yellow lentils, oval shaped and flat, are the split form of whole moong, with a markedly different taste. They are often prepared as a side dish for vegetarian meals. Moong dhal should maintain their shape when cooked, like separate grains of rice.

As a variation, moong dhal can also be made into a thick dhal or soup which is eaten with warm roti.

Whole Green Moong/Mugh

These dark green oval lentils have a mild aromatic flavour which is enhanced by introducing a pinch of hing/asafoetida during cooking.

Under the name of mung bean, moong has received worldwide acclaim as a health food. When sprouted it is highly nutritious, especially when eaten raw.

Red Kidney Beans/Raima Beans

These dark red kidney shaped beans are a particular favourite in Bengal and the Punjab. You can prepare them in the same manner as whole moong.

They can be boiled with onions, a few cinnamon sticks and salt and served with a generous blob of butter.

Soya Beans

Soya beans are highly nutritious. They are used to produce tofu or fresh soya bean curd. Textured protein or TVP is a popular soya bean product.

Tempeh, another soya bean product is semi fermented and is used in Far-East cooking and has excellent proteins.

Tur *or* Toover *Dhal*/Oil Dhal

A yellow lentil with a natural oil content. Delicious with rice.

Urad Dhal

A small white lentil used often in vegetables.

Black Gram

Little black lentils used in place of brown lentils.

VAAL NI DHAKHOO – THICK BEAN SOUP

Serves 6 — Time : 120 mins

375 ml (11/2 c) split vaal beans (dried beans), soak overnight
1 medium onion, chopped
2 medium tomatoes, chopped
5 ml (1 t) ginger, crushed
5 ml (1 t) garlic, crushed
5 ml (1 t) red masala
7 ml (11/2 t) salt
10 ml (2 t) lemon juice
5 ml (1 t) sugar
Coriander leaves
30 ml (2 t) oil
5 ml (1 t) asafoetida
1 dry red chilli

Cook beans with onion for 1 to 11/2 hours, adding enough water to form a thick soup.

Whisk with egg beater.

Add tomatoes, ginger, garlic, turmeric, masala, salt, lemon juice and sugar.

Use another saucepan and heat oil.

Add dry chilli and heat for a few seconds.

Then add asafoetida and bean mixture.

Beat with egg whisk until semi smooth.

Cook on low heat for 20 minutes.

Serve on a portion of rice – pour over rice, or in individual bowls as soup.

A thick soup to serve with rice. Use any dried bean.

PALAK DHAL – SPINACH DHAL

Serves 4 — Time : 1 Hour

250 ml (1 c) tur dhal
4-5 medium chopped tomatoes
11/4 ml (1/4 t) turmeric
3-4 green chillies
250 g coarsely chopped spinach
Salt
11/4 ml cumin/jeero seeds
21/2 ml (1/2 t) ginger, chopped
21/2 ml (1/2 t) garlic, chopped
21/2 ml (1/2 t) black gram
1 red chilli
11/4 ml (1/4 t) hing/asafoetida

Cook the dhal until it is soft in a pressure cooker.

When the dhal is cooked place the tomatoes, turmeric, chillies, spinach and salt into the pressure cooker.

Cook the dhal mixture until the tomatoes and spinach are soft.

Cook cumin seeds in hot oil in a pan until they splutter.

Place the other spices into the pan.

Place the spice mixture with the dhal mixture in the pressure cooker.

Stir.

KABULI CHANNA – WHOLE CHICKPEA

Serves 4 Time : 1 hr 30 mins

500 ml (2 c) whole chickpeas/whole Kabuli Channa
3 t oil
2 medium onions, chopped
2 t cumin seeds
2 t ginger chopped finely
1 t garlic crushed
2 t chilli powder
1 t turmeric powder
2 t ground cumin
30 g tamarind, soak, remove pips and use pulp
6 chopped tomatoes
1 t sugar
1 t gharam masala
1/2 t black pepper
Salt to taste
2 sliced green chillies
1 bunch of chopped fresh coriander
1 sliced lime or lemon
1 medium onion in rings

Soak chickpeas in hot water overnight.

Pressure cook the chickpeas in salted water until it is soft.

Heat oil in a pan and fry onions until golden brown.

Add ginger, garlic, cumin seeds, turmeric powder, chilli powder and cumin powder.

Continue frying for a couple of minutes, add the tomatoes and sugar into the pan.

Cook for 5 minutes.

Stir in tamarind pulp, chickpeas and salt into the pan.

Cook for 10 to 15 minutes on low heat.

Take out a few channas, mash them and put them back into the mixture to thicken the sauce.

Serve in individual bowls.

Garnish with fresh coriander, sliced lime or lemon, green chillies and onion rings.

This wholesome chickpea dish, Kabuli Channa is a firm family favourite. A Punjabi speciality served with large puffed puri (Indian bread).

CREAMED LENTILS

Serves 4 Time : 90 mins

250 ml (1 c) black gram, washed
21/2 ml (1/2 t) turmeric powder
2 cm piece of ginger, chopped fine
1 sliced green chilli
Bay leaves
5 ml (1 t) salt
2 chopped tomatoes
125 ml (1/2 c) beaten yoghurt
Ghee
1 sliced onion
21/2 ml (1/2 t) chilli powder
125 ml (1/2 c) cream
Lemon juice

Soak the washed black gram for a couple of hours.

Place the turmeric, ginger, chilli, bay leaves and salt into the pot with the lentils and cook until the lentils are cooked.

Place the yoghurt and the tomatoes with the lentil mixture and mix well.

Cook the onion in some hot ghee until golden brown.

Place the chilli powder into the onion mixture and cook for 2 minutes.

Place the onions, cream and lemon juice into the lentil mixture and mix.

"Sekta-ni-sing", the most popular lentil-toovar dhal, cooked with Indian drumstick.

SPROUTED *MOONG* – SPROUTED GREEN LENTILS

Serves 4 | Time : 60 mins

Overnight soaking, 1 to 2 days for sprouting

250 ml (1 c) moong (green lentils)
1 medium onion
1/2 t mustard seeds
1/2 t turmeric
1 green chilli
1/4 t hing/asafoetida
1 t gharam masala
1 t sugar
1 T grated coconut (dessicated coconut may be used)
Salt
3 T oil

Sort and wash moong *thoroughly.*

Soak moong *overnight in hot water.*

Drain the next day and keep tied in cloth until the sprouts appear. This would take 1 or 2 days.

Heat oil in pan and put mustard seeds into the boil.

When the seeds splutter put 2 or 3 pieces of green chilli, hing and the turmeric into the pan.

Add onions and cook for 2 to 3 minutes

Add the moong *and cook for a few minutes.*

Put in 1 cup of water and the gharam masala.

Cook on low heat until dry and soft.

Put in the coconut, the sugar and the salt.

Cook for a few minutes and remove from heat.

Garnish with fresh coriander.

Serve sprouted moong *with fried puri (Indian bread) and onion salad.*

TOOVER NI DHAL WITH SEKTA NI SING — LENTIL DHAL WITH DRUMSTICKS

Serves 4 | Time : 45 mins

250 ml (1 cup) toover/tur dhal/oil lentils
500 ml (2 cup) boiling water
750 ml (3 cup) warm water
1 medium onion, chopped
2 sekta ni sing or 2 Indian drumsticks – peeled and cut into pieces – (Optional)
100g pumpkin, cubed
15 ml (1 tsp) fresh ginger, pounded
5 ml (1 tsp) turmeric
5 ml (1 tsp) salt
7 ml (1.5 tsp) sugar
10 ml (2 tsp) lemon juice
2 ml (1/2 tsp) methi/fenugreek seeds
8 limri/curry leaves
2 tomatoes, grated

Vagaar Spices

2 ml (1/2 tsp) hing / asafoetida powder
1 whole dried red chilli
40 ml (2 1/2 tsp) cooking oil or ghee

Garnish

15 ml (1 tsp) dhunia/coriander leaves, chopped

Sort the lentils and soak in the boiling water for 30 minutes.

Rinse the lentils several times and place in pot with the warm water, onion, drumsticks and 15 ml (1 tsp) oil. Cover pot and simmer on medium heat until contents form a thick soup (about 40 mins).

Add remaining ingredients to pot and whisk well with eggbeater until smooth.

In another small pot, heat remaining oil and brown the chilli before adding the other vagaar spices.

Quickly pour over the lentils, cover with lid and simmer for 15 minutes.

Garnish with chopped coriander leaves.

Sekta ni sing or drumsticks are delicious when cooked with lentils. This dhal is always served over a helping of rice, with spiced vegetable dishes like green peas, green beans or brinjals. With rice, it forms the staple diet in India. Dhal may also be served as a thick soup with hot toast in winter. Mango pickle and papadums are a traditional accompaniment.

MASOOR NI DHAL – SPINACH RED LENTIL CURRY

Serves 6 | Time : 30 mins

400 g (2 c) red masoor lentils
1 onion, chopped
3 cloves of garlic, sliced
8 curry leaves
2 green chillies, sliced lengthwise
2 ml (1/2 t) turmeric
5 ml (1 t) salt
100 g spinach, shredded
15 ml (1 t) oil
5 ml (1 t) mustard seeds

Wash lentils and drain.
Bring 750 ml (3 c) of water to boil in a saucepan.
Add lentils, onion, garlic, curry leaves, chillies, turmeric, salt, spinach and 15 ml (1 t) oil.
Cover saucepan and cook for 15 minutes.
Heat remaining oil in a small saucepan.
Add mustard seeds and brown.
Pour this over the lentil curry.
Stir and gently simmer for 10 minutes.

This lentil can be served with puri (bread), chapattis and a sweet dried fruit pickle. It can also be served over cooked rice and with onion and carrot pickle. It makes a superb cold winter's night soup and an easy preparation for a nutritious meal.

Red lentils make a wholesome and delicious curry when cooked with spinach and onions. It thickens into a gray which is versatile as it can be served with breads or rice.

MOONG GREEN LENTILS

Serves 6 plus 20 minutes soaking | Time : 1 hr

375 ml (1 1/2 c) green moong lentils
750 ml (3 c) boiling water
1 large onion, chopped
5 ml (1 t) red masala
2 ml (1/2 t) fresh ginger, pounded
5 ml (1 t) salt
2 ml (1/2 t) turmeric
1 large ripe tomato, grated
5 ml (1 t) lemon juice
45 ml (3 t) cooking oil
1 dried red chilli
1 ml (1/4 t)) hing / asafoetida powder
5 ml (1 t) jeero / cumin seeds

Garnish

30 ml (2 t) dhunia / coriander leaves, chopped

Sort moong lentils, wash several times and soak in water for 20 minutes.
Drain and place in deep saucepan.
Add 750 ml boiling water, cover and boil rapidly for 15 minutes.
Add onions, cover again and cook on medium heat for about 20 minutes until lentils are soft.
Stir to prevent sticking.
Add red masala, ginger, salt, turmeric, tomato and lemon juice and mix well.
The moong will reduce to a thick gravy.
Use an eggbeater to whisk the moong into a semi-smooth consistency.
In another large saucepan, heat oil and add chilli and asafoetida.
Then add the moong mixture to the pot, cover, lower heat and simmer for 10 to 15 minutes.
Garnish with coriander leaves.

DHAL-E-DHODI – SPLIT CHICKPEA DHAL

Serves 4 – 6   Time: 1 hour plus 30 minutes soaking

500 ml (2 c) chana dhal/split chickpea lentils
1 large onion, chopped
Flesh of 1 gem squash* OR
125 ml (1/2 c) chopped dhodi/Indian marrow
15 ml (1 t) cooking oil
1 tomato, chopped
2 ml (1/2 t) red masala
2 ml (1/2 t) fresh ginger, pounded
2 ml (1/2 t) fresh garlic, pounded
7 ml (1 1/2 t) salt
5 ml (1 t) lemon juice
5 ml (1 t) turmeric
10 ml (2 t) dhunia/jeera/coriander-cumin powder
45 ml (3 t) cooking oil
5 ml (1 t) jeera/cumin seeds OR
2 sticks cinnamon, 50 mm each
1 small dried red chilli

Garnish

Chopped dhunia/coriander leaves

Sort the lentils on a tray, removing husks, etc.

Wash well and soak in plenty of warm water for about 30 minutes.

Boil 1 l water in a saucepan with lid and add the lentils, onion, chopped gem squash and oil.

Cover with lid and simmer for 45 minutes until the lentils are soft but retain their shape.

Add tomato and seasonings and stir well.

Heat the oil and brown the chilli and cumin seeds or cinnamon sticks.

Add the lentil mixture, lower heat and simmer for 20 minutes.

Garnish with coriander leaves.

*Note If you find it difficult to peel the gem squash, boil it with the lentils, then scoop out the flesh (omitting seeds) and mix it through.

"Dhal-e-Dhodi", a Gujerati speciality, dhal cooked with Indian marrow.

A table with different types of continental bread: garlic herb bread, sesame rolls, white and brown bread and pizza.

Home Baked Breads

Breads from the East:
Chapatis - unleavened Indian bread
Paratha
Spinach stuffed parathas
Grilled tandoori naan
Puri - puffed bread

Roomali roti
Kulcha foolka - Fried yeast bread
Poora - spiced pancakes
Savoury soya loaf
Countrystyle homemade bread

Dosa - South Indian pancake
Sambar - South Indian gravy
Breads of the world:
Wholewheat bread
Sesame herb rolls
French bread, garlic bread, herb bread
Italian pizza - vegetarian pizza

Tomato chutney
Unusual eastern toppings for pizza
Greek pita bread
Middle East style bread - Schwarma

Tacos - Super Mexican bread
Mexican corn tortillas

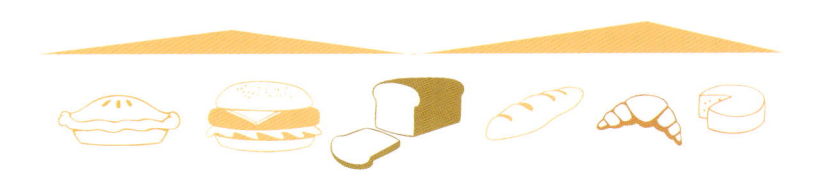

CHAPATTIS (ROTIS) – UNLEAVENED INDIAN BREAD

Serves 4   Time : 45 mins

500 ml (2 c) flour (brown, wholewheat or white)
5 ml (1 t) salt
90 ml (6 T) melted ghee
140 ml (1/2 c) hot water or oil
60 ml (1/4 c) melted butter for spreading

Sift flour and salt. Rub in 90 ml butter or ghee with fingertips to a fine texture. Bind into a pliable dough with water. Knead on board for 2 to 3 minutes.

Divide dough into 8 portions. Roll each portion between palms to form balls.

Using lightly floured surface roll one ball to a 7,5 cm circle or disc. Spread 5 ml (1 t) melted butter on the tip. Make a few fingertip imprints. Spread lightly with flour. Lift and gather the edges to form an air pocket. Press edges together and press flat.

Roll this round gently and evenly to a 15 cm diameter disc. The chapatti can be turned over when being rolled. A lightly floured surface will ease the rolling. Place aside on a tray.

Repeat with remaining balls. Heat a tari (an Indian griddle) or a heavy pan on a hot plate. Place the chapatti in the pan and allow to cook on both sides ts lightly brown colour. The wet look of the chapatti will disappear and it will have a freckled appearance.

Remove from pan, spread 5 ml (1 t) of ghee on either side and place in a covered container. Cook remaining chapattis.

Serve warm or cool with any Indian dish.

To warm, place each chapatti on a heated pan for a few seconds on either side. A pile of chapattis can be wrapped in foil and placed in a heated oven to keep warm.

Dough can be kept in the refrigerator for 3 days. This dough freezes well for up to 3 months.

PARATHA – (Variation)

A triangular shaped paratha may also be made from basic roti/chapatti dough.

Make 1 basic roti dough. Divide dough into three balls.

Roll one portion of dough to a large round the size of a dinner plate.

Spread with 1 t melted ghee, sprinkle with flour and make fingertip imprints.

Fold your round paratha in half.

Spread 2 t melted ghee over this half, sprinkle with flour and then fold in half again, forming a triangular shape.

Roll into a large triangle and cook as chapattis.

No vegetarian dish can be complete without a serving of homemade roti or chapattis.

Chapattis are the most popular Indian bread. It makes a perfect accompaniment with dishes which have a thick gravy. Chapattis are flat, round flaky breads made of flour and ghee dough. They are cooked on an Indian griddle called a tari. The Indian rolling pin is dainty, long and tapered at the ends. The widest part is hardly 25 mm in diameter.

Because of the ghee content, it may not be too wise to prepare this too often – especially when on a reducing or health diet. The ghee or fat contents can be brought down to a minimum.

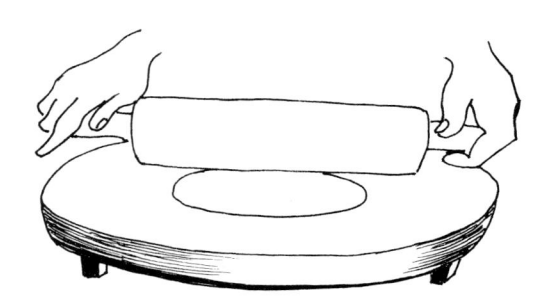

SPINACH STUFFED *PARATHAS*

Serves 6 Time : 1hr 30 mins

Fresh spinach filling

1 bunch spinach, remove stalks and
chop 300 g chopped spinach
250 g cream cheese
1 small tomato, chopped
30 ml (2 t) butter or ghee
15 ml (1 t) mustard seeds
3 ml (1/2 t) hing/asafoetida
7 ml (1 1/2 t) salt
7 ml (1 1/2 t) freshly ground black pepper
3 ml (1/2 t) turmeric

Heat ghee in saucepan. Add mustard seeds and hing. Add tomato and toss for a few minutes. Add spinach and toss for 7 minutes until moisture evaporates. Add cheese, salt and pepper.

Toss for a few minutes and leave on a low heat to obtain a moist free consistency. Remove from heat and cool.

Basic *Paratha* dough (bread)

250 ml (1 c) brown flour
375 ml (1 1/2 c) cake flour
100 ml melted butter/ghee
200 ml hot water
5 ml (1 t) salt

   A. Hand made dough
      Sift flour, add salt, rub in ghee and bind with water to make a soft, firm dough.

   B. Food processor dough
      Place flour and salt into processor and sift by running machine for 10 seconds. Pour in ghee. Allow 10 seconds run. Add hot water and run blade for 5 seconds until dough comes clear of sides.

To Stuff *Parathas*

Divide dough into 12 pieces and form balls. Roll each ball into a 15 cm round. Place 30 ml (2 t) of spinach filling onto half the round. Bring the other half of the round over and press to form a half round shape. Press outer edge firmly, fold over again to form a Paratha or triangle shape, press edges firmly. Press Paratha on edges for a neat finish flattening slightly. Repeat using up the filling with remaining dough.

To fry

Heat 750 ml (3 c) oil in a 20 cm saucepan. This allows for semi deep frying. Fry two Parathas at a time to a golden brown. Fry on a medium heat. Drain well and serve with a slice of lemon and sweet pickle.

A recipe from the hills of Mount Abu, Rajastan, India. Parathas are typical Indian breads. Eaten on cold nights, it has nurtured the tummies of even the hungriest of men. These parathas provide the nutrients and vitamins that only garden fresh spinach and cheese can offer.

GRILLED *TANDOORI NAAN*

Serves 6 Time : 2-3 hrs

500 g flour (plain)
5 ml (1 t) salt
5 ml (1 t) baking powder
30 ml (2 T) oil
10 g instant dried yeast
180 ml (3/4 c) yoghurt
180 ml (3/4 c) warm water

Sift flour, salt and baking powder.

Add oil and dried yeast, and mix well.

Bind into a sort dough with yoghurt and water.

Knead until satiny and pliable and roll into a little oil to keep from sticking.

Place in a bowl and cover with cling wrap.

Allow to rise to double its size.

Preheat oven to 200°C.

Divide into 6 and shape into a tear drop, measuring 20 cm x 12 cm.

Heat a baking tray.

Slap onto tray.

Bake for 2-3 mins.

Turn on grill and brown the naan until it bubbles into a golden puffed naan.

Serve hot.

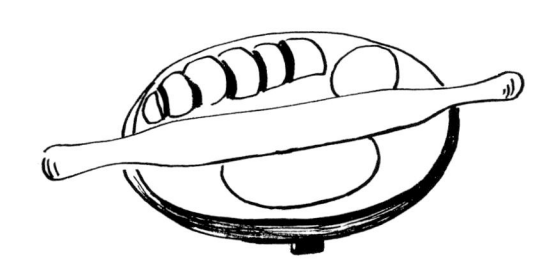

Roomali roti. Nothing is more fascinating than to watch an expert flying a piece of dough from hand to hand swirling it in the air to create a masterpiece- a roomali roti. In the forefront- Tandoori roti, paratha, puri and roomali roti.

PURI – PUFFED BREAD

Serves 6   Time : 45 mins

500 ml (2 c) cake flour
100 ml (6 t) melted ghee
5 ml (1 t) salt
150 ml (1/2 c) hot milk and water, equal portions
750 ml (3 c) oil for deep frying

Sift flour, add salt, rub in ghee using the fingertips and bind into a pliable dough with hot liquid.

Use as hot water as your fingers can bear as this maintains a very light dough.

Knead dough well, incorporating air into it as you knead. Allow to stand for 15 minutes.

Divide in 20 small balls. Roll each ball in the palm of your hand to ensure a perfect round.

Press on board and roll to 2,5 mm thickness and 80 mm in diameter.

Heat oil in a deep saucepan till hot.

Slide 3 rounds in at a time.

Press lightly to immerse into the oil for a second.

The puri dough should puff completely.

Immediately turn over and cook for further 1 minute.

Fry puri is very quick, no more than 3 minutes.

Drain puri well on absorbent paper.

Serve hot or cool.

To reheat place on baking tray in 180° C oven till warm. Surprisingly, puris remain puffy for hours.

Use as a bread or it can also be filled with any vegetable curry.

As for tea, spread apricot jam over and enjoy this rich delicacy.

A delightful easy deep fried bread to serve with a vegetable tarkhari.

Variation Batura

Make a puri dough, but divide only into 6 balls. Roll into 6 large puri. Each batura is a large round puri. Serve with Kabuli Chana.

ROOMALI ROTI

Serves 4   Time : 15 mins

The making of roomali roti has to be seen to be believed. I watched with amazement at the performance. Roomali roti demands a technique which only an experienced pair of hands can perform. Roti or chapatti dough is rolled into a round. Then the performer of the art niftily throws the roti from one palm of his hand to the next in rhythmic movement. In quick continuous movement the roti grows into a bigger round. The artist swirls the roti deftly into the air for a few seconds, swirls it again and again until the shape expands to twice the size of a dinner plate before your eyes. Cooking roomali roti is for outdoors as an inverted karhai or Indian pan is placed over a coal burner. The roti is slapped onto the hot pan for cooking. Seconds later, little golden bubbles appear. The cook casually throws and flips the roti over to brown on the other side. Perhaps, roomali roti should only be made by the experts.

KULCHA – FOOLKA (FRIED YEAST BREAD)

| Serves 8 | Time : 60 mins + rising |

1 kg bread flour, sifted
30 ml (2 T) cooking oil
60 ml (4 T) melted ghee
15 ml (3 t) jeero / cumin seeds
5 ml (1 t) salt
10 ml (2 t) dried yeast
250 ml (1 c) lukewarm water
15 ml (1 T) sugar
750 ml (3 c) cooking oil for frying

Rub the 30 ml oil, the ghee, cumin seeds and salt into the flour with your fingertips.

Add the yeast to the lukewarm water with the sugar.

To ensure that the yeast is working, leave it for 10-15 minutes until it has frothed.

Make a hole in the centre of the flour mixture and pour in the yeast.

Bind with extra lukewarm water into a soft sticky dough.

Place the dough in an airtight container and allow to rise for 4-8 hours.

Roll out to 5 mm thickness and cut into rounds approximately 50 mm in diameter, using a biscuit cutter.

Deep fry for a few seconds in hot oil, until light brown on both sides.

The **foolka** should puff completely in the oil.

POORA – SPICED PANCAKES

| Serves 8 | Time : 60 mins |

750 ml (3 c) bread flour
200 ml (3/4 c) cornflour or maize flour
200 ml (3/4 c) chana flour
5 ml (1 t) green masala
12 ml (2 1/2 t) salt
2 ml (1/2 t) fresh ginger, pounded
2 ml (1/2 t) fresh garlic, pounded
5 ml (1 t) turmeric
125 ml (1/2 c) coriander leaves, finely chopped (fenugreek herbs can also be used)
1,6 l (4 1/4 c) water
125 ml (1/2 c) cooking oil

Sift flour into large bowl and mix spices, salt and herbs into flour with your fingers.

Make a thin mixture by adding 1 l (4 c) water to make a flowing mixture.

Heat **tavi** (griddle) on medium to high heat.

Using fork and onion as a brush, coat **tavi** well with oil.

Take 1/2 c of mixture and pour around the edges of the pan, forming a large thin pancake. The mixture usually flows to the centre of the **tavi**, so tilt the pan to form a full round pancake.

Cook for 2 minutes or until the edges of the pancake begin to curl and separate from pan.

Lift and turn over.

If pancake breaks when lifting, allow to cook for a little longer.

Cook second side for 2 minutes also.

Remove and spread lightly with butter.

Delicious spicy pancakes to savour with any dish.

SAVORY SOYA LOAF

| Serves 6 | Time : 1 hr 15 mins |

120 g soya mince, flavoured or plain
250 g self raising flour, sifted
250 g whole wheat flour, sifted
2 ml (1/2 t) baking powder
45 ml (3 T) parsley, chopped
5 ml (1 T) buttermilk
5 ml (1 t) salt
5 ml (1 t) chopped green chillies
5 ml (1 t) chopped garlic
2 ml (1/2 t) turmeric

Mix all the ingredients together in a bowl. Combine well.

Place the mixture into two greased bread tins.

Bake at 160°C for 1 hour or until cooked through.

When the loaves are removed from the oven, they must stand for 5 minutes and then be turned out onto a cooling rack.

The loaf can be served hot or cold with a salad.

COUNTRY STYLE HOMEMADE BREAD

| Serves 6 and 2 hrs or more for rising | Time : 1 hr |

1 l (4 c) flour
15 ml (1 T) oil
5 ml (1 t) salt
10 ml (2 t) sugar
5 g instant yeast
400 ml (1 1/3 c) lukewarm water

Sift flour and salt. Add sugar and oil. Rub into flour. Add yeast, mix well and bind into a dropping consistency with water.

Place into a greased loaf tin. Allow to rise double its size.

Bake in pre-heated oven of 180°C for 40 to 50 minutes or until brown on top.

A recipe which my daughters delight in making. The recipe has become part of our country lifestyle. Enjoy the fresh aroma of baked bread that permeates the kitchen.

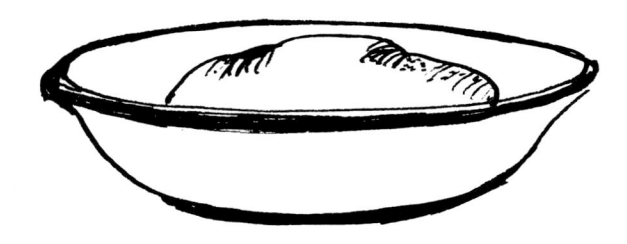

A large paper dosa. The South Indian traditional breakfast served with a spicy potato filling and fresh coconut chutney.

DOSA – SOUTH INDIAN PANCAKE

Serves 6　　🕐 Time : 60 mins
overnight standing

500 ml (2 c) rice flour
250 ml (1 c) chana flour (lentil flour)
5 ml (1 t) salt
15 ml (1 T) yoghurt
5 ml (1 t) jeera/cumin, crushed
750 ml (3 c) cold water
85 ml (1/3 c) cooking oil

Sift flour into a bowl. Season with salt, cumin and mix well with yoghurt.

Add water, 1 cup at a time to make a thin batter.

Stir well and cover.

Leave overnight.

Heat a well seasoned pan or griddle.

Spread a layer of oil around the pan.

Pour about 1/3 c batter on a pan starting from the center.

Oil the edges of the pancake.

Cover with a lid and cook gently for about 2 minutes.

Flip dosa over.

Cook a little and remove.

Make remaining dosa.

To serve, prepare spicy mash potatoes and use as a filling.

Delicious with coconut chutney and sambar*.

* See recipe opposite.

SAMBAR – SOUTH INDIAN GRAVY

Serves 6　　🕐 Time : 45 mins

250 ml (1 c) toover dhal / oil lentils
1 carrot cut into fine cubes
125 ml (1/2 c) small cutbeans
125 ml (1/2 c) brinjals, cubed
125 ml (1/2 c) tamarind juice (make juice by soaking a small piece, 1T tamarind fruit in 1/2 c hot water.
Work flesh away from pips. Remove pips. Strain juice).
10 fresh curry leaves
Salt to taste – 1 t
5 ml (1 t) chilli powder
15 ml (1 t) oil
5 ml (1 t) mustard seeds
1 ml (1/4 t) hing/asafoetida

Boil lentils in 2 1/2 c water.

Add vegetables, tamarind juice, curry leaves, salt and chilli powder.

Heat oil in another pot. Add mustard seeds and hing. Allow to pop, then add and mix well with boil lentils.

Cook further 15 minutes. Serve warm in small bowls.

SPICY MASH POTATOES

Serves 6　　🕐 Time : 60 mins

6 potatoes (medium)
60 ml (1/4 c) oil
1 t chopped garlic
2 green chillies
1 t mustard seeds
2 onions sliced
Lemon juice & coriander leaves

Boil and mash 6 potatoes until smooth. Season with salt.

Heat 1/4 c oil (60 ml) in a pan. Add 1 t garlic chopped. Fry 2 chopped green chillies. 1 t mustard seeds. Add 2 sliced onions and fry until golden brown

Stir in mash and mix well on a low heat until dry, cooking away excess moisture.

Garnish with 2 T lemon juice and 1/2 c dhunia leaves.

WHOLEWHEAT BREAD

| Serves 4 | ⌚ Time : 1 hr 30 mins 2 hours rising time |

500 ml (2 c) white bread flour
500 ml (2 c) nutty wheat
10 ml (2 t) salt
30 ml (2 T) stamped sunflower seeds
30 ml (2 T) linseed
45 ml (3 T) wheat germ
15 ml (1 T) honey
10 ml (2 t) dried yeast
30 ml (2 T) oil
625 ml (2 1/2 c) warm water

Sift flour, salt and add linseed, wheat germ and sunflower seeds.

Mix honey into 1/2 glass of warm water.

Add yeast and let it stand for 10 to 15 minutes until the mixture reaches the top of the glass.

Add to dry ingredients and mix into a wet dough and add the rest of the water.

Lastly, add oil and knead very well.

Place in a well greased bread tin.

Place two pieces of cling wrap on top of the tin and seal well. Let it stand to rise for about two hours.

Bake for 1 hour in 200°C oven.

An excellent health bread which is extremely popular.

SESAME HERB ROLLS

| Serves 6 | ⌚ Time : 90 mins and rising |

750 ml (3 c) flour
10 g instant yeast
125 ml (1/2 c) yoghurt
250 ml (1 c) lukewarm water
15 ml (1 T) sugar
5 ml (1 t) salt
80 ml (1/3 c) melted butter
5 ml (1 t) oregano
7 ml (1 1/2 t) basil leaves
15 ml (1 T) chopped parsley
2 ml (1/2 t) hing
2 ml (1/2 t) thyme
30 ml (2 T) sesame seeds

Sift the flour. Add the salt, spices, herbs and sugar. Mix well. Add the dry yeast and mix again.

Pour in the melted butter and mix. Bind with the yoghurt and the lukewarm water. Make a soft, sticky dough.

Allow dough to stand until it rises to double its size. This usually takes 2 1/2 to 3 hours.

Punch down and divide into 36 balls.

Grease a patty pan and place 3 balls in each – to make a clover shape. Sprinkle with sesame seeds.

Allow to rise.

Bake in preheated oven – 180°C for 15 to 20 minutes until golden brown.

This splendid recipe is unusual in flavour. Herbs of your choice may be added.

FRENCH BREAD

| Serves 4 | Time : 60 mins + rising |

Makes 4 small loaves.

1 kg (8 c) cake flour
15 ml (1 T) salt
10 ml (2 t) sugar
10 g instant dry yeast
15 g butter or margarine
500 ml (2 c) warm water

Combine the salt, sugar and flour together. Place the yeast into the bowl and mix in.

Using your fingers rub the butter into the dry ingredients. Slowly mix the warm water into the mixture to make a soft dough. Knead the dough until it becomes elastic and smooth.

When kneaded place the dough on a surface which has been floured lightly and cover with damp muslin cloth and let it stand for 15 minutes.

Beat down the dough. Divide dough into four. Make 4 equal sized, thin, long loaves from the dough. Place on a baking tray which has been greased. Make diagonal cuts on the tops of all the loaves.

Place damp muslin cloth over the loaves and place in a warm place to rise for about 25 to 30 minutes. The dough should be double in size.

Remove cloth. Brush the loaves with water. Bake for 20 to 25 minutes at 220°C.

GARLIC BREAD

| Serves 4 | Time : 15 mins |

1 loaf of French bread
250 ml (1 c) soft butter
10 ml (2 t) crushed garlic

Cut the loaf into slices leaving the bottom uncut so that the loaf still holds together.

Cream butter and garlic until smooth.

Spread generously on both sides of each slice.

Wrap in foil and bake for 15 minutes in preheated oven of 200°C.

HERB BREAD

| Serves 4 | Time : 15 mins |

1 loaf of French bread
250 ml (1 c) soft butter
125 ml (1/2 c) chopped herbs or 10 ml (2 t) dried mixed herbs

Follow the same instructions as for Garlic Bread.

Pizza

The Italian Pizza may be a vegetarian's treat specially with the exotic toppings available.

| Serves 2 | 🕒 Time : 1 hr 15 mins |

Dough

500 ml (2 c) sifted self raising flour
5 ml (1 t) salt
250 ml (1 c) buttermilk
15 ml (1 T) butter

Mix flour and salt together. Add the butter and rub into the flour until the flour looks like very fine bread crumbs.

Add the buttermilk and mix into a soft dough. Divide into two.

Roll out to 6 mm thickness on a floured surface.

Place the pizza round onto a greased tray and cover with tomato chutney or tomato sauce with any topping.

VEGETARIAN PIZZA

1 quantity tomato chutney, see opposite
250 ml (1 c) mushrooms, sliced
125 ml (1/2 c) green pepper
6 pitted olives
1 tomato
1 onion
250 ml (1 c) mozzarella cheese or strong flavoured cheese
A pinch oregano
A pinch of thyme
Salt and pepper to taste
30 ml (2 T) mint sauce, optional

Spread tomato chutney over dough. Smother with sliced mushrooms, sliced green peppers, olives, onion rings, sliced tomato, thyme, oregano, salt, pepper and grated cheese.

For extra delight spread with mint sauce.

Bake in preheated oven of 180°C for 20 minutes.

TOMATO CHUTNEY

| Serves 4 | 🕒 Time : 20 mins |

4 large ripe tomatoes, grated
62 ml (1/4 c) oil
5 ml (1 t) crushed garlic
5 ml (1 t) crushed ginger
5 ml (1 t) chilli powder
2 ml (1/2 t) salt
2 medium onions, sliced
5 ml (1 t) mint
10 ml (2 t) sugar
10 ml (2 t) mint sauce or coriander chutney
15 ml (1 T) tomato paste
10 ml (2 t) ground cumin

Heat the oil. Add the garlic, ginger, chilli powder and the onions.

Fry for a few minutes until the onions are golden brown. Add the remaining ingredients.

Cook until the oil separates from the chutney. Some water can be added if required.

Cool and use to top pizza.

This cooked tomato chutney makes a good basic sauce for any vegetable. The green chilli, ginger and garlic gives it an Eastern flavour.

UNUSUAL EASTERN TOPPINGS FOR PIZZA

| Serves 4 | Time : 15 mins |

Coconut-cream sauce

1/2 quantity tomato chutney
125 ml (1/2 c) coconut, grated
125 ml (1/2 c) cream
125 ml (1/2 c) grated cheese

Mix the coconut and the cream into the tomato chutney mixture. Spread over pizza dough. Cover with cheese and bake.

Peanut sauce

1/2 quantity tomato chutney
125 ml (1/2 c) crushed peanuts
125 ml (1/2 c) grated cheese

Mix the peanuts into the tomato chutney mixture. Spread over pizza dough. Cover with cheese and bake.

Chilli pizza – Hot but delicious!

1/2 quantity tomato chutney
2 red chillies, chopped
125 ml (1/2 c) grated cheese

Cover the pizza dough with chutney. Spread with grated cheese and chopped chillies.

Green pepper pizza – Also hot, but excellent

1/2 quantity tomato chutney
1 green pepper, chopped
1 tomato
2 fresh green chillies
125 ml (1/2 c) grated cheese

N.B. Mozzarella is the preferred cheese for pizza toppings.

GREEK PITA BREAD

| Serves 8 | Time : 1 hr 30 mins 2 hours for rising |

25 g instant dried yeast
750 ml (3 c) lukewarm water (more may be added if needed)
15 ml (1 T) sugar
1 kg wholewheat flour
10 ml (2 t) salt
75 ml (5 T) olive oil (salad oil may also be used)

Combine the flour and the salt. Add the yeast mixture to the flour. Mix well.

While kneading add water to make a firm dough, add the oil to the dough gradually while it is being kneaded. Place the kneaded dough which must be greased all over into a large oiled bowl.

Place the bowl into a warm spot. Cover with a damp cloth and leave it to rise until double its size. When the dough has risen remove from the bowl and knead again for a few minutes.

Divide the dough into 16 parts. Press each dough ball onto a floured surface either with a rolling pin or by hand until it is 15 cm in diameter.

Place each dough round between two floured cloths. Place in a warm area and allow to rise. Preheat oven to 220°C.

Heat several greased baking sheets for a few minutes. Place the dough onto the trays and bake in the middle of the oven for about 10 minutes.

Pita is delicious with saucy dishes and dips.

This bread of Greek origin puffs whilst baking, making it perfect for filling.

MIDDLE EAST STYLE BREAD (SCHWARMA)

Make a delicious Middle East Schwarma by filling Pita Bread with the following:

Mix 2 c chopped cabbage with 3 T salad cream, 2 chopped tomatoes, 1 chopped onion, 1 1/2 t chopped garlic, 2 T parsley, 1 t salt.

Chill and fill in Pita Bread for a tasty cold lunch.

Mexico, the land of very tasty spicy dishes. Foreground- Guacomole- an avocado dip, and a plate of nachos. At the back, pawpaw salad and the main platter of tacos with beans filling.

TACOS – SUPER MEXICAN BREAD

Serves 18　　Time : 2 hrs

320 ml (1 1/4 c) maize flour
250 ml (1 c) cake flour
15 ml (3 t) oil
180 ml (3/4 t) salt
3 ml (1/2 t) ground black pepper
3 ml (1/2 t) chilli powder
Bind with cold water
750 ml (3 c) oil for frying

Mix flour with oil, salt, spices and enough cold water to make a soft dough.

Keeping your fingers lightly oiled, divide into 18 small balls. Roll each ball on a floured surface to 10 cm in diameter.

Heat oil in a large pan to moderate temperature. Slide one tacos in and cook until semi firm.

Now using a knife, lift one side of the tacos and bend in half, suspending the top on the blade of another knife. By doing this you will create a shell to hold the filling.

Cook on the other side. Remove, drain and cool. Fill with the following.

Filling for Tacos (See Tomato Soya Mince Recipe)

Each tacos shell should be filled with a heap of vegetable protein (soya mince), a scoop of tinned chilli or baked beans, a helping of shredded lettuce, chopped onion and tomato salad, and smother with cream cheese, sour cream or grated cheese.

Deliciously designed to fill the hungriest tummy.

MEXICAN CORN TORTILLAS

Serves 12　　Time : 15 mins

2 cups masa farina or fine maize flour
2 T oil
1 1/4 – 1 1/3 cups warm water

Rub oil into flour. Season with a pinch of salt. Combine flour with warm water to make a dough which holds together. Shape dough into a ball with your hands. Divide the ball of dough into 12 equal parts. Roll each part into a ball of dough.

To shape the dough use two cloths which have been wrung dry after being dipped into water. Place a slightly flattened ball of dough between the cloths.

Roll lightly and evenly with a rolling pin until the diameter of the cake is 6 inches. Pull cloths back carefully and place cake between two sheets of waxed paper.

To cook, take off the top layer of waxed paper carefully. Place the uncovered side of the cake onto an ungreased, preheated medium to hot griddle or a frying pan on medium to high heat. Peel off other waxed sheet as cake becomes warm.

Cook for 11/2 to 2 minutes, turning often, until cake looks dry and lightly spotted with brown speckles.

The tortilla should be soft and will briefly puff up.

Serve immediately or store when cool in an airtight container.

A selection of snacks from the East.

Delectable Snacks, Savouries and Dips

Tasty dips
Popular cheese of the world
Dhodi moothia - green marrow dumplings
Thika ghathia - Potato gram noodles

Savoury banana fritters
Sev - savoury noodles
Kashmiri cutlets
Easy potato cutlets - tikkies
Chilli bites (gateaux piments - Mauritian style)
Spring rolls

Tasty Dips

Dip	Ingredients	Method and Suggestions
Apple and mint dip	3 large green apples, peeled and cored, liquidise with 3 T water, 1/2 c fresh mint, 2 t sugar, 1/2 green chilli, 1 t salt, 2 t cumin.	Serve with croutons (fried bread cubes) or potato chips.
Avocado dip	1 medium ripe avocado, 1/4 t salt, 1/4 t green chilli, chopped finely, 1/4 t crushed garlic, 1 1/2 T drinking yoghurt.	Scoop avocado flesh into a bowl of a food processor. Add remaining ingredients and mix well until smooth. Serves 4 Time 15 minutes. Serve with salty biscuits or corn chips.
Brinjal dip	1 large brinjal, sliced, 3 T oil, 1/4 t asafoetida, 1/2 t chilli powder, 1/2 t salt, 1 t lemon juice.	Place brinjal under grill till soft and brown. Mash flesh until smooth. Heat oil. Add seasonings. Brown for a few seconds. Mix in brinjal pulp. Cool and serve with wholewheat bread.
Butter bean dip	1 c butter beans, tin beans may be used, mash until smooth, 1 t chopped basil leaves, dried may be used, 1 T oil, a pinch of asafoetida, 1/2 t salt, 1/2 t sugar, 1 T tomato puree.	Heat oil, brown asafoetida. Add tomato purée, salt, sugar and braise. Add beans and cook for 10 minutes. Cool and serve with crusty bread.
Cream cheese dip	250 g cream cheese, 1/2 c grated cheddar cheese, salt and pepper to taste. 1 tomato chopped, 1/2 green pepper chopped, 1/2 chopped onion, 1/4 c chopped herbs, 2 T milk.	Mix well. Serve with steamed vegetables e.g. cauliflower, baby corn, celery, carrots and mushrooms. Serve with potato crisps.
Cucumber and cheese dip	1 c grated cucumber. Squeeze out moisture. Mix with 250 g cream cheese, 1 t mustard powder, 1/2 t salt, a pinch of turmeric, 1/2 green chilli, chopped finely. Sprinkle with chilli powder.	Mix well together. Garnish with a sprinkling of red chilli powder. Serve with cheese biscuits.
Guacamole Mexican avocado dip	2 large avocadoes pulped, 1 green chilli chopped, 2 T chopped coriander leaves, 1/2 t sugar, 1/2 t crushed garlic, 1/2 tomato chopped, 1 t salt, 1/2 t black pepper, 2 T chopped onion.	Mix together. Serve with corn chips, raw silvers of carrots, cucumbers and celery.
Hot coriander and tomato dip	2 C coriander herb, 1 ripe tomato, 1/2 green chilli 1/2 t salt, 4 cloves garlic, 1 T lemon juice, 1 t cumin seeds.	Blend ingredients in food processor. Serve with garlic bread.
Houmos – Lebanese dip	1 1/2 C cooked chickpeas, 2 T salad oil, 1 T lemon juice, 1 T tahini paste or 1 T sesame seeds, 1 T yoghurt, 1 t salt.	Place in blender till smooth. Serve with pita bread or french bread.
Oriental cheese dip	1 c creamed cottage cheese, 2 T salad cream, 2 T chopped pickle onions, 1 T apricot jam 1/2 t ground ginger, 1 T flaked almonds, 1 1/2 T soya sauce, 1/2 t chopped parsley.	Mix well and serve with papadums or potato chips.
Pineapple dip	1/2 C creamed cottage cheese, 3 T sour cream, 1/2 C chopped tin pineapple, 1 T chopped mint, 1/2 t sugar, 1/4 t salt.	Blend well and serve with savoury biscuits.

Popular Cheese of the World

Bel Paese
An Italian cheese, rather mild and sweet.

Brie
A French soft cheese covered with a firm crust. Tangy and sometimes runny.

Camembert
Based from Normandy, France. Danemark makes Camembert *as well.*

Danish Blue
A Danish blue veined cheese.

Edam
A Dutch semi-hard mild cheese. Covered with a bright red skin.

Emmenthal
A mild Swiss cheese very much like Gruyère.

Gorgonzola
An Italian cheese with a strong smell. This is a blue veined cheese.

Gouda
A creamy coloured Dutch cheese with superb flavour for cooking.

Gruyère
A Swiss cheese, firm with large holes in the cheese. Ideal for eating and cooking.

Mozzarella
An Italian cheese rather soft and mild, used for pizza.

Parmesam
An Italian cheese, very strongly flavoured making it perfect for cooking. Grates easily for toppings.

Ricotta
An Italian cheese for lasagna.

Feta
Milk cheese excellent for Greek salads.

Sweet milk
A soft cheese with a mild flavour.

DHODI MOOTHIA – GREEN MARROW DUMPLINGS

Serves 6 — Time: 60 mins

500 g grated dhodi marrow
185 ml (3/4 c) mealie meal
125 ml (1/2 c) chana flour, sifted
60 ml (1/4 c) bread flour
5 ml (1 t) green masala
2 1/2 ml (1/2 t) red masala
5 ml (1 t) ginger
30 ml (2 T) melted ghee
1 ml (1/4 t) bicarbonate of soda
5 ml (1 t) jeera/cumin
5 ml (1 t) salt
2 1/2 ml (1/2 t) turmeric
10 ml (2 t) dhunia/jeera (coriander/cumin) powder
125 ml (1/2 c) milk

Squeeze all the water out of the dhodi.

Mix all the ingredients together to form a soft dough.

Place the dough into a baking dish and place into an oven preheated at 180°C.

Bake for 20 to 30 minutes.

THIKA GHATHIA – POTATO GRAM NOODLES

Makes 700 g — Time: 90 mins

500 g chana flour
1 potato, boiled and mashed
15 ml (1 T) salt
10 ml (2 t) chilli powder
Coarsely ground black pepper
60 ml (1/4 c) oil
1/4 c water for thick mixture

Place all the ingredients together and mix well.

Put the mixture through a noodle machine using the plate with the largest hole.

Fry in hot deep oil.

The heat must however not be too hot.

SAVOURY BANANA FRITTERS

Serves 4 — Time: 90 mins

125 ml (1/2 c) chana flour
125 ml (1/2 c) self raising flour
5 ml (1 t) chilli powder
5 ml (1 t) salt
5 ml (1 t) crushed large aniseed (soomph or varyari)
4-6 bananas, sliced
Oil for deep frying
Chilli powder for sprinkling
Water for thick mixture

Combine the flour, the chilli powder, salt and aniseed with water to make a thick mixture.

Dip the bananas into the mixture and deep fry until golden brown.

Sprinkle with chilli with powder.

Serve with chutney.

Green bananas can be used for a more tangier flavour. This delicious snack is easy to prepare.

SEV – SAVOURY NOODLES

Makes 500 g — Time: 45 mins

3 C (750 ml) chana flour
10 ml (2 t) fine salt
10 ml (2 t) black pepper or chilli powder
2 ml (1/2 t) baking powder
3/4 c water

Use same method as in Potato Gram Noodles, using the finest hole plate in the noodle machine.

KASHMIRI CUTLETS

Serves 6 — Time : 120 mins

500 g potatoes boiled peeled and mashed
30 ml (2 T) semolina
125 ml (1/2 c) sliced carrots
125 ml (1/2 c) sliced green beans
125 ml (1/2 c) peas
30 ml (2 T) ghee
1 sliced onion
5 ml (1 t) gharam masala
5 ml (1 t) ground jeera/cumin
1 sliced green chilli
3 cm chopped piece of ginger
15 ml (1 T) sultanas
125 ml (1/2 c) chopped mixed nuts
Yoghurt
15 ml (1 T) milk
2 1/2 ml (1/2 T) saffron
1 beaten egg
Bread crumbs

Mix the semolina and the potato together.

Boil the vegetables until cooked yet firm.

Cook the onion in hot ghee until golden brown. Place the gharam masala, the jeera, the chilli, the ginger, salt and vegetables into the pan with the onions.

Cook until the juice is evaporated. Combine the sultanas and nuts and cook gently.

Combine with the yoghurt and saffron.

Take the potato mixture and gently roll into a rectangular shape.

Place a little of the potato aside before rolling the mixture out. Place the vegetables onto the potato. Place the nuts and sultana mixture in the middle of the vegetables.

Roll the potato up and use the left aside potato to seal the potato roll and close any holes.

Using a brush cover the roll with beaten egg then sprinkle bread crumbs all over.

Cook in a oven either as it is or with foil wrapped around it.

It is cooked when it is golden brown.

Serve with chutney or curry.

Variations

EASY POTATO CUTLETS (TIKKIES)

Serves 6 — Time : 45 mins

500 g potatoes – boiled and mashed
1 C stale bread – soaked in water to soften
2 t salt
3 large chillies chopped finely
4 t cumin seeds crushed coarsely
1/2 c chopped coriander or mint leaves

Remove excess moisture by squeezing the soaked bread.

Season with salt.

Add the other ingredients.

Mix to a firm dough.

Form small balls, press down lightly and fry 4 at a time in shallow oil until golden brown.

Serve with a dhunia/coriander chutney.

In China, food is served piping hot and is eaten with chopsticks. In the forefront- corn soup and spring rolls. Middle- fried rice and vegetable noodles. Soya, garlic, and chilli sauce are usually served as accompaniments.

CHILLI BITE – *GATEAU PIMENT*
Mauritian delicacy

Serves 8   Time : 60 mins

500 g chana dhal – split chickpea
2 t chopped green chilli
1 t salt
1 t turmeric
3 t crushed aniseed
3 t coriander leaves, chopped
4 T green onion, chopped finely
1/2 t baking powder
3 c oil for deep frying

Soak dhal overnight in hot water. Next day drain and crush finely in a food processor or crush by hand in a stone mortar and pestle. Add chilli, salt, turmeric, aniseed, coriander leaves, green onions and baking powder. Mix well to form a wet dough.

Heat oil in a deep saucepan or indian wok. Make small balls and drop into oil. Gently fry for a few minutes until golden brown and cooked inside.

Eat with a chilli sauce. Eaten in true Mauritian style, a french bread stuffed with gateau piment is enough to fill a hungry tummy.

SPRING ROLLS

Serves 4   Time : 60 mins

12 spring roll skins
500 ml (2 c) shredded cabbage
1 carrot cut thinly into strips
125 ml (1/2 c) fresh green beans cut into thin strips
1/2 green pepper cut into strips
62 ml (1/4 c) celery, chopped
80 ml (1/3 c) sesame oil or salad oil
5 ml (1 t) crushed garlic
Soya sauce to taste
Oil for deep frying

Vegetable filling

Heat 10 ml (2 t) oil in a pan.

Fry garlic, toss in cabbage and stir fry for three minutes.

Add 10 ml (2 t) soya sauce whilst frying.

Remove cabbage with a perforated spoon.

Heat 15 ml (1 T) oil in pan and stir fry remaining vegetables separately as with cabbage.

Mix all vegetables and set aside.

Season with soya sauce if necessary.

To make spring rolls place 15 ml (3 T) of vegetable filling in the centre of a pastry skin.

Fold up sides and make a tight roll.

Stick down the outer edge with a little flour and water paste.

To fry

Heat oil in a wok and deep fry spring rolls a few at a time until golden.

Re-heat and crispen in hot oil again just before serving.

Serve with chilli sauce.

Chilli sauce

Combine 125 ml (1/2 C) water with 30 ml (2 T) salad oil, 45 ml (3 T) white vinegar, 2 chopped chillies, 15 ml (3 t) sugar and a pinch of salt. Mix well and shake before serving.

Fresh coconut chutney being stonepounded and pressed into a very fine, smooth texture.

Fresh Chutneys, Pickles and Sauces for Snacks

Spiced soya sauce
Hot tamarind sauce
Garlic chilli sauce
Tomato sauce home style
Fresh coriander chutney
Cucumber carrot chutney

Apple and mint chutney
Coconut chutney
Peanut and curry leaf chutney
Mango pickle
Mixed fruit pickle

SPICED SOYA SAUCE

| 10 helpings | Time : 15 mins |

250 ml (1 c) soya sauce
1 heaped teaspoon maizena cornflour
15 ml (1 T) oil
5 ml (1 t) crushed garlic
1 green chilli, chopped
15 ml (1 T) chopped green onion

Heat oil in pan.
Add garlic and chilli.
Mix maizena into soya sauce.
Add to pan with onion.
Cook for 10 minutes.
Cool and serve with snacks.

GARLIC CHILLI SAUCE

| Serves 4 | Time : 10 mins |

60 ml (1/4 c) cooking oil
125 ml (1/2 c) water
30 ml (2 T) sugar
125 ml (1/2 c) white vinegar
5 ml (1 t) fresh garlic, pounded
5 ml (1 t) green masala
5 ml (1 t) salt

Place ingredients in mixing bowl and beat with a rotary beater until well blended. Bottle and store in the refrigerator.

A tangy sweet-and-sour dressing to pour over fried rice or tossed salads, or to use as a dip for freshly fried chilli bites. Try it also with chicken in batter.

HOT TAMARIND SAUCE

| 10 helpings | Time : 20 mins |

250 ml (1 c) tamarind juice
15 ml (1 T) tomato sauce
30 ml (2 T) grated carrots
5 ml (1 t) cumin, crushed
5 ml (1 t) chilli powder
5 ml (1 t) sugar
2 ml (1/2 t) salt
30 ml (2 T) mint, chopped or 15 ml (1 T) mint sauce

To make tamarind juice soak 250 ml (1 C) tamarind in 375 ml (11/2 c) warm water.
Loosen fruit from pips and strain thickened tamarind sauce through sieve.
Use strained liquid and mix all ingredients and store in bottle.

TOMATO SAUCE HOME STYLE

| 10 helpings | Time : 15 mins |

250 ml (1 c) tomato sauce
5 ml (1 t) mustard seeds
10 fresh curry leaves
5 ml (1 t) chilli powder
5 ml (1 t) sugar
2 ml (1/2 t) salt
15 ml (1 T) oil

Heat oil in pan.
Add mustard seeds and curry leaves.
Brown, then add remaining ingredients.
Cook for 10 minutes.
Cool and bottle.

A lady from Kerala grating a fresh coconut with an old-fashioned handpiece.

FRESH CORIANDER CHUTNEY

| 12 helpings | Time : 20 mins |

500 ml (2 c) washed coriander leaves and stems
10 ml (2 t) cumin seeds
5 ml (1 t) salt
2 ml (1/2 t) crushed garlic
1/2 tomato
Juice of one lemon

Blend till smooth.
Serve with savories, samoosas and snacks.

COCONUT CHUTNEY

| Serves 6 | Time : 45 mins |

500 ml (2 c) fresh coconut
125 ml (1/2 c) coriander or mint leaves
30 ml (2 t) lemon juice
1 large green chilli
A small piece of ginger 1 cm square
4 cloves of garlic
5 ml (1 t) salt
45 ml (3 T) water

Blend ingredients till smooth.
*Serve with **dosas** and snacks.*

CUCUMBER CARROT CHUTNEY

| Serves 4 | Time : 20 mins |

125 ml (1/2 c) grated cucumber
125 ml (1/2 c) carrots
30 ml (2 T) chopped onion
1 green chilli, chopped
2 ml (1/2 t) salt
Juice of half lemon

Blend till smooth and serve with snacks.

PEANUT AND CURRY LEAF CHUTNEY

| Serves 4 | Time : 45 mins |

100 g peanuts
1 T chopped coriander leaves
1/2 tomato
1 ml (1/4 t) salt
2 ml (1/2 t) crushed garlic
10 ml (2 t) cumin seeds
5 g or a handful of curry leaves
Juice of one lemon

Blend well together.
Serve with snacks.

APPLE AND MINT CHUTNEY

| Serves 6 | Time : 20 mins |

See Apple and Mint dip – snacks section page
Serve with snacks.

MANGO PICKLE

> Preparation time : 45 minutes
> 4 weeks for standing

2 kg green mangoes
500 ml (2 c) salt
200 g methi seeds pounded to powder
100 g mustard seeds
60 ml chilli powder
45 ml (3 T) turmeric
15 ml (1 T) hing / asafoetida powder
250 ml (1 c) cooking oil for mixing
750 ml (3 c) cooking oil for pickling

Wipe mangoes with a wet cloth. Cut into eight pieces lengthwise and place in a large dish.

Make spice mixture with salt, methi seeds and mustard powder, chilli powder, turmeric and asafoetida.

Add 250 ml oil and mix well into spices. Rub the mixture over the mango pieces. Place the mangoes in a clean jar and seal well.

On the third day pour the 750 ml oil over the mangoes, covering them completely. Leave pickle to stand for 4 weeks before serving.

A traditional Mango Pickle which can be stored for a long period.

Variations

SWEET MANGO PICKLE

1kg half ripe mangoes – grated

Make a syrup with 2 C sugar, 1 C water.

Season with 2 t salt, 2t chilli powder, 2 cinnamon sticks.

A few strands of saffron.

Cook mangoes in syrup until soft and thick.

MIXED FRUIT PICKLE

> Preparation time : 45 minutes
> 5 days for standing

1 kg mixed dried fruits
125 ml (1/2 c) malt vinegar
15 ml (3 t) mustard powder
15 ml (3 t) chilli powder
250 ml (1 c) oil
15 ml (3 t) turmeric
20 ml (4 t) salt
8 cloves of garlic peeled and cut in half
5 ml (1 t) cloves
1 large cinnamon stick
15 ml (3 t) black peppercorns
125 ml (1/2 c) golden syrup or 1 cup homemade syrup/honey

Wipe dried fruits with a damp cloth and slice each piece of fruit into strips about 6 mm in thickness and place in a mixing bowl.

Place vinegar into a cup and stir in mustard and chilli powder.

Add the vinegar mixture and remaining ingredients to the dried fruits and mix thoroughly.

Place into a pickle jar and allow to rest for 5 days.

This sweet pickle is ideal to serve with vegetable and lentil dishes.

Home made syrup is a marvellous way to preserve fruit and serve as pickles. Pickles are important to any vegetarian meal. Dried fruit blended with golden syrup and spices makes an exceptional sweet.

For sweet lovers - strawberry cheesecake, appletart and trifle.

Irresistible Desserts, Puddings, Ice cream and Sweetmeats

Cheesecake with strawberry topping
Burfi
Cottage cheese pudding - seekhund
Easy cheese pudding - seekhund
Milk cheese balls in syrup - Rasgoola
Nutty khulfi ice cream with vermicelli
Sweet semolina pudding
Milk pudding
Delicious ginger tart
Almond and nut sweetmeat - badami halwa
Warm carrot dessert - gajar halwa
Quick and easy trifle
Iced fruit salad
Easy creamy vanilla ice cream
Nutty ice cream
Ice cream sundaes, sauces and toppings
A variety of ice creams

CHEESECAKE WITH STRAWBERRY TOPPING

Serves 8   Time : 2 to 3 hrs

3/4 crushed tennis biscuits – 4 T melted butter
395 g can condensed milk
250 g cream cheese
50 ml (1/5 c) lemon juice
250 ml (1 c) sour cream
10 ml (2 t) gelatine
25 ml (5 t) water
410 g can strawberries
15 ml (1 T) custard powder

Combine with the biscuit crumbs and the melted butter together. Place it into a pie dish and press down to make an even crust and chill. Mix together the condensed milk and cream cheese.

Gradually add the lemon juice while stirring the mixture. Add the sour cream.

Dissolve the gelatine in water on a low heat. Slowly place the gelatine into the mixture stirring contiuously.

Place the mixture into the crust and allow to set by chilling the cheesecake.

Drain the can of strawberries, placing the syrup aside. Combine the custard powder with a little of the strawberry syrup. Place the rest of the syrup into a saucepan and mix in the custard powder mixture.

Boil the syrup up until the syrup becomes thick. Take saucepan off the heat and add the strawberries. Mix with a spoon until pulpy. Let the syrup cool.

Spread the strawberry syrup over the cheese filling. Chill until firm enough to slice.

CREAMY *BURFI* SWEETMEAT WITH SOME DELECTABLE FLAVOURS

Serves 4-6   Time : 45 mins

Basic recipe makes 10 small blocks

250 g milk powder
1 small tin of cream or 250 ml (1 c) of fresh cream
150 g icing sugar
5 ml (1 t) cardamom seeds, crushed
30 ml (2 T) chopped almonds
125 ml (1/2 c) water
15 ml (1 T) ghee

Mix milk powder with half the cream using fingertips. Create a crumby texture. (You may want to place in a food processor for just a few seconds).

Make a syrup by boiling the water for 3 minutes. Stir in icing sugar. Boil for a further 3 minutes. Mix in milk powder and stir constantly for 8 minutes on a low heat. Add remaining cream, ghee, cardamom and 15 ml (1 T) almonds and cook for another 2 minutes.

Grease a small square dish with ghee. Pour in the burfi mixture. Sprinkle with remaining almonds or chopped pistachios and a sprinkling of cardamom seeds. Allow to set overnight. Cut in diamond shapes and store in a cool area.

STRAWBERRY *BURFI*

Serves 4-6   Time : 45 mins

Make 1 basic **burfi** *recipe as above but change the following :*

Flavour with 60 ml (4 T) strawberry milk shake powder.
Use 60 ml (4 T) less icing sugar. Pour 2 ml (1/2 t) strawberry essence into syrup whilst cooking. Garnish with chopped almonds coloured pink (to colour almonds, drop a few drops of pink liquid food colour over almonds, rub in well and dry in a warmer drawer).

CHOCOLATE *BURFI*

| Serves 4-6 | Time : 45 mins |

Make 1 quantity of basic burfi, *using 30 ml (2 T) less icing sugar. Add 15 ml (1 T) cocoa, 5 ml (1 t) strong coffee into syrup whilst cooking. Follow recipe and decorate with almonds flakes.*

CHOCOLATE TOPPED *BURFI*

| Serves 4-6 | Time : 45 mins |

Make 1 quantity of basic burfi. *Melt 200 g cooking chocolate in a double boiler. When chocolate is liquid pour over burfi and allow to semi set. Just before chocolate hardens, cut in squares then allow to set till firm.*

ALMOND *BURFI*

| Serves 4-6 | Time : 45 mins |

Make 1 basic quantity of burfi *but use 125 ml (1/2 c) of almond powder (make this by grinding almond flakes in a coffee grinder). Also remove 125 ml (1/2 c) of milk powder used in the recipe. Follow basic recipe.*

PEPPERMINT *BURFI*

| Serves 4-6 | Time : 45 mins |

Make 1 basic quantity of burfi *but add 2 ml (1/4 t) green food colouring to syrup whilst boiling. Garnish with green coloured almonds.*

SAFFRON AND PISTA *BURFI*

| Serves 4 | Time : 40 mins |

Make 1 basic quantity of burfi *adding 5 ml (1 t) saffron strands and 30 ml (2 T) chopped pistachios to syrup. Decorate with a few strands of saffron, pure silver edible paper (warq) and a few silvers of pistachios.*

COCONUT *BURFI*

| Serves 4-6 | Time : 45 mins |

Make 1 basic quantity of burfi *removing 125 ml (1/2 c) of milk powder. Add 125 ml (1/2 c) freshly shredded coconut or 125 ml (1/2 c) dessicated coconut.*

COTTAGE CHEESE PUDDING (*SEEKHUND* SPECIAL)

| Serves 6 | Time : 90 mins |

250 ml (1 c) cream cheese
1 litre homemade curd
250 ml (1 c) castor sugar
30 ml (2 T) chopped almonds
5 ml (1 t) crushed cardamom seeds
One drop of egg yellow colouring

To decorate

1 sprinkling of pistachio nuts (shelled and chopped)

A few strands of saffron

How to make curd?

Time : 2 days to set, 1 day to drain

1 litre milk
30 ml (2 T) powdered milk
15 ml (1 T) buttermilk

Place milk into a pot and mix powdered milk. Bring to the boil and cool to body temperature. Mix in yoghurt and place in an enamel dish to stand for 2 days until thick.

Take a colander and line with fine cotton or muslin cloth. Pour the thickened milk into colander and tie cloth. Allow to stand for 1 day until a solid curd is formed.

To make seekhund

Time : 90 minutes

Line a tray with newspaper. Cover with cotton cloth and spread cream cheese over. Allow to stand for 1 hour.

Finally place cream cheese, curd, almonds, cardamom and castor sugar into a food processor and pulse quickly until well blended. Add just a drop of colour to give a tinge of yellow and pulse once more.

To Serve

Place in a large glass crystal bowl. Top with pistachios and saffron strands. Seekhund is traditionally served as a first course in an individual bowl with a fried puri. After dinner a dessert as exquisite as this will add that finality to your menu.

A rather involved procedure but the best ever seekhund is produced.

EASY COTTAGE CHEESE PUDDING – (*SEEKHUND*)

| Serves 6 | Time : 30 mins |

500 g cream cheese
125 ml (1/2 cup) castor sugar
5 ml (1 t) nutmeg grated
5 ml (1 t) cardamom seeds, crushed
10 ml (2 t) almonds, chopped
3 drops of egg yellow colouring
A few silvers of almonds or Pistachio nuts
A few saffron strands

Mix cream cheese, sugar, nutmeg, cardamom seeds, chopped almonds and food colour. You may put the mixture into a food processor to mix well.

Place the cheese in a beautiful cut glass bowl. Decorate with saffron strands and nuts.

Serve chilled with fried Indian Puri, or with any exotic fruit of your choice e.g. sliced mango, kiwi fruit, paw paw, sweet melon carved into balls or shapes.

RASGOOLA – MILK CHEESE BALLS IN SYRUP (BENGAL)

Serves 3-4 Time : 2 hrs
plus 4 hours for cheese to dry

Cheese

1 litre (4 c) milk
20 ml (4 t) lemon juice
15 ml (1 T) flour or semolina
2 ml (1/2 t) baking powder

Syrup

250 ml (1 c) sugar
1 litre (4 c) water
Few drops rose or vanilla essence

Cheese

Bring milk to boil in a saucepan. Add the lemon juice and stir. Remove from heat and leave to stand for 15 minutes. The milk should curdle, leaving a clean whey. Pour off whey and tie the milk cheese in a muslin cloth or bag. Suspend it until the rest of the whey has dripped out. (This takes up to 4 hours). The cheese should be completely dry and solid. A weight may be placed on the muslin bag if all the whey has not dripped out.

Remove cheese from cloth and knead to a soft paste with the flour and baking powder. Roll the paste into balls the size of large marbles.

Syrup

Boil the water, sugar and essence in a saucepan for 30 minutes. When the syrup is slightly sticky and begins to bubble, gently lower the cheese balls into the saucepan. Cover and cook over low heat for 7 minutes. Turn the balls over and cover again. After 15 minutes, remove lid and swing saucepan with a circular movement, then cover again. Repeat for about 45 minutes until the balls are soft and spongy. (They remain white).

Serve warm in small bowls with the syrup.

Variation – Rasmalai

Serve the cheese balls cold in a cream made by boiling 2 litres (8 c) milk until reduced to half quantity. Flavour with 125 ml (1/2 c) sugar, 5 ml (1 t) crushed cardamom seeds and 5 ml (1 t) rose essence.

Bengal is famous for this sweetmeat. Even though making rasgoola is a lengthy business and the sweet is extravagantly rich in calories, I find it totally irresistible.

NUTTY KHULFI ICE CREAM WITH VERMICELLI

Serves 4-6 Time : 60 mins
Freezing time : 2-3 hrs

1 1/2 (6 c)litres milk
375 g condensed milk
30 ml (2 T) cornflour
30 ml (2 T) cold milk
85 g (1/2 c) sugar
30 ml (2 T) water
22 ml (1 1/2 T) silvered almonds
15 ml (1 T) pistachios or other nuts, chopped
30 ml (2 T) extra fine vermicelli
2 t butter
1/3 c sugar

Using a heavy bottom saucepan, bring the milk and condensed milk to heat. Stir well and allow to simmer for 20 minutes.

Using the cold milk, make a smooth paste with the cornflour, then add 125 ml (1/2 c) of the warm milk to it. Stir, then add to the milk in the saucepan. Stir again and simmer for about 30 minutes, until thick.

A thin film of milk may form at the top – just stir onto the mixture as this occurs. Remove from heat.

In a small pot mix sugar and water and bring to the boil rapidly until it turns caramel. Remove from the heat. Allow to cool and stir into the milk mixture.

Pour into the freezer container and allow to semi-freeze. When it is semi-gold, remove from freezer and stir well again mixing in half the nuts and cornflakes. Freeze until solid.

Prepare vermicelli for serving.

Heat 1 c water, add 1/3 sugar, 2 t butter. Bring to boil then add vermicelli and cook for 10 minutes. Serve hot or cold.

Serve in individual bowls with a helping of vermicelli. Decorate with nuts and cornflakes.

An outstanding dessert to relish.

KHULFI VARIATIONS

Serves 4 Time : 1hr 10 mins

Chopped fruit, grated chocolate or a sprinkling of fine sweets, make pleasant decorations. A touch of rose syrup over the top is absolutely delicious.

Prepare Basic Khulfi *without nuts and cornflakes. In place of these add following when making :*

Saffron Kesar *Khulfi*

Add 2 t saffron powder or 1 t saffron strands

Kaju Cashew *Khulfi*

Add 1/2 cup chopped cashew nuts

Elaichi (Cardamom) *Khulfi*

Add 2 t crushed freshly roasted cardamom seeds and 1 t rose essence

Chocolate *Khulfi*

Add 2 t cocoa to ice cream and 1 heaped teaspoon of strong instant coffee, and 1 t vanilla essence

Mango *Khulfi*

Add 1 cup of fresh mango pulp to khulfi.

SWEET SEMOLINA PUDDING – (SOOJI)

Serves 6 Time : 30 mins

250 ml (1 c) semolina (tasty wheat)
3/4 c melted ghee
15 ml (1 T) almond flakes
15 ml (1 T) sultanas
250 ml (1 c) sugar
250 ml (1 c) warm milk
375 ml (1 1/2 c) warm water
5 ml (1 t) crushed cardamom seeds
2 ml (1/2 t) grated nutmeg

Heat ghee in a heavy saucepan. Braise semolina on a low heat tossing for 15 to 20 minutes. This time consuming process is necessary to keep this pudding from getting sticky or lumpy. A low heat will maintain light shade. Semolina should not brown at all.

Add almonds and sultanas and braise for 5 minutes. Add water and milk, previously heated.

Stir cover saucepan and allow to cook on low for 10 minutes. Add sugar, cardamom and nutmeg and stir up with fork. Cook for a few minutes.

Sooji *is traditionally served warm as a starter with a Gujerati meal. Delicious to serve as a pudding at the end of any meal.*

There is nothing boring about this pudding.

MILK PUDDING

Serves 6 — Time : 80 mins

125 g butter
4 1/2 c milk
3/4 c maizena
3/4 c sugar
1/4 C golden syrup
1/2 t fine elachi/cardamom

Melt butter in a large pot. Add milk and bring to boil.

In a separate bowl mix maizena, sugar, syrup, and elachi together.

Take 1 cup milk (from boiled milk) and mix well into maizena mixture so that there are no lumps. Pour the mixture into the pot with boiled milk and mix well. Keep pot on the plate and keep stirring until mixture thickens like custard. Take off heat.

Pour into tray and sprinkle with khas khas.

Bake at 220°C for 15 to 20 minutes until golden brown on top.

When cool cut and keep in fridge.

DELICIOUS GINGER TART

Serves 6 — Time : 60 mins

250 ml (1 c) self raising flour
30 ml (2 T) sugar
125 ml (1/2 C) butter
30 ml (2 T) water

Ginger filling:
130 ml (1/2 cup) sugar
310 ml (1 1/4 C) water
5 ml (1 t) ground ginger
30 ml (2 T) custard
A pinch of salt

To Serve

1 cup fresh cream to pour over if preferred.

Preheat oven to 180°C.

Sift flour, add sugar, rub in butter and bind in dough with 2 T water.

Grease a pie dish with butter.

Line with dough. Prick dough with fork to make several insertions, otherwise the dough will rise too much. Alternatively 2 cups of dried beans can be placed on the dough to keep the pastry flat whilst baking. Bake for 15 minutes.

Meanwhile, make ginger filling by boiling sugar and water for 15 minutes. Add custard powder, ginger and salt.

Stir and pour into baked pastry crust.

Bake for 15 minutes at 180°C till done.

Serve warm with fresh cream.

BADAMI HALWA – ALMOND & NUT SWEETMEAT

Serves 6-8 plus 12 hours setting   Time : 2½ hrs

Syrup

800 g sugar
300 ml (1 1/4 c) water
10 ml (2 t) lemon juice
125 ml (1/2 c) cornflour, dissolved in
900 ml (3 3/4 c) water
125 ml (1/2 c) sago, soaked in 500 ml (2 c) cold water for 30 minutes and drained
2 ml (1/2 t) red and 2 ml (1/2 t) yellow colouring

or

5 ml (1 t) green colouring
125 ml (1/2 c) ghee, solidified
150 g blanched almonds, split
30 g pistachio nuts
30 g charoli/chirongee nuts (optional)
1 whole jaiphul/nutmeg, grated
10 ml (2 t) elaichi/cardamom seeds, crushed
1 ml (1/4 t) saffron strands

Syrup

Dissolve sugar in the 300 ml water in a large, heavy saucepan. Add lemon juice, bring to the boil for 15 minutes. Do not stir.

Dissolve the cornflour in the 900 ml water and add to the syrup with sago and colouring. Cook, stirring continually, for 1 hour.

Stir in ghee 15 ml (1 t) at a time, mixing well with each addition. Cook for another 45 minutes. By this time the halwa should come away from the sides of the saucepan without sticking. Add the nuts, nutmeg, cardamom and saffron to the halwa and stir. Cook for 15 minutes.

Pour into a greased dish 20 cm square and allow to set for 12 hours. Cut into 40 mm squares.

To Store

Wrap in foil and store in airtight container for 4 to 6 weeks.

A brightly coloured sweetmeat consisting of almonds and other nuts set in a base of saffron syrup thickened with sago and ghee.

GAJAAR HALWA – WARM CARROT DESSERT (PUNJAB)

Serves 4   Time : 1hr 10 mins

750 g carrots
100 g butter or ghee
30 ml (2 T) silvered almonds
200 ml (3/4 c) sugar (or less to taste)
250 ml (1 c) milk
125 ml (1/2 c) fresh cream
7 ml (1 1/2 t) elachi/cardamom seeds, crushed
30 ml (2 t) pistachio nuts, chopped finely
250 ml (1 c) fresh cream, whipped

Peel carrots and grate finely (use a food processor).

Melt butter in a heavy saucepan, add the silvered almonds and toss for 1 minute. Add the carrots and stir for about 10 minutes over a higher heat. Blend in sugar, milk and the 125 ml cream and stir with a wooden spoon.

Leave the saucepan uncovered and simmer over medium heat for 20 minutes until all the moisture evaporates. Mix in cardamom seeds and half the pistachios. Simmer for 10 minutes, stirring occasionally with a fork to separate the carrot shreds. The halwa should be soft and moist; the quantity of carrots will however reduce as moisture evaporates.

Serve warm in individual bowls and decorate with remaining pistachio nuts and the whipped cream.

Standing out boldly on vegetable stalls in India are heaps of stout and bright red carrots. (Quite unlike the South African variety, Indian carrots are far sweeter and more vividly coloured).

The luscious carrot halwa which I relished in India was an experience to remember. The carrots blend beautifully with the nutty flavour of almond and pistachios gently cooked in butter, cream and milk, creating an unusual and easy dessert which never fails to impress. I serve it warm in cut-glass bowls, dressed with a generous helping of cream and topped with extra pistachios. It may also be served as a cold sweet.

Carrot halwa takes time to prepare, but you can safely get on with other tasks while it simmers away. It may be prepared several days in advance and reheated gently. It also freezes well.

Festivals are a way of life in the East. These delectable sweetmeats are part of the tradition. Lying in the front, are different flavoured barfis, halwa, magaj, delicious rasgoolas and jalebi.

QUICK AND EASY TRIFLE

| Serves 8 | Time : 40 mins |

1 sponge sandwich cake
1 large tin sliced peaches
250 ml (1 C) strawberry jam
500 ml (2 C) cooked custard
250 ml (1 C) fresh cream, whipped
45 ml (3 T) chopped walnuts
15 ml (1 T) chopped glaze cherries

Slice cake into 3 rounds or layers.

Spread jam over each layer and sandwich together.

Cut into 1 cm cubes.

Place into 8 individual serving bowls.

Top each layer with juice from sliced peaches.

Pour over a layer of custard, cream, peaches and decorate with nuts and cherries.

Variation

Serve with a helping of jelly.

ICED FRUIT SALAD

| Serves 6 | Time : 60 mins plus freezing |

90 g cream cheese
30 ml (2 t) cream
15 ml (1 t) brown sugar
125 ml (1/2 c) mayonnaise
Salt
Lemon juice
125 ml (1/2 c) chopped glace cherries
250 ml tinned pineapple
125 ml (1/2 c) tinned cherries
125 ml (1/2 c) chopped nuts
250 ml (1 c) whipped cream
Strawberries

Mix the cream cheese with the 30 ml of cream.

Mix the lemon juice, sugar, mayonnaise and salt with the cream cheese mixture.

Add the cherries, the nuts and the fruit to the mixture.

Add whipped cream and gently mix by folding it into the mixture.

Place into a tray and freeze.

Do not stir while freezing.

When the salad is frozen, slice and serve with nuts or fresh strawberries.

EASY CREAMY VANILLA ICE CREAM

| Serves 6 | Time : 35 mins + freezing |

1 litre (4 c) full cream milk
310 ml (1 1/4 C) sugar
4 ml (3/4 t) salt
30 ml (2 T) vanilla essence
1000 ml (4 C) fresh cream, whip just before freezing

Rinse a saucepan, leaving wet, add half the milk.
Add heat until warm.
Dissolve sugar and salt.
Pour in remaining milk.
Allow to semi freeze.
Now add vanilla essence and stir in whipped cream.
Whisk well and freeze.

NUTTY ICE CREAM

| Serves 4 | Time : 20 mins |

90 g brown sugar
120 g butter
90 ml (6 T) evaporated milk
10 ml (3/4 T) golden syrup
Vanilla ice cream
Chopped nuts

Mix sugar, butter, milk and syrup in a pot which is over boiling water. Mix for 5 minutes.
Allow the fudge sauce to cool.
Place a spoon of ice cream into a parfait glass.
Place a little fudge sauce and some nuts on top of the ice cream.
Continue until the glass is filled.
Place a cherry on the top of the ice cream dish.

Ice Cream Sundaes, Sauces and Toppings

A creamy ice cream can be turned into a supreme sundae by just topping with one of the following sauces. Scoop two generous balls of your homemade ice cream onto an oval dessert plate. Place a fresh spring of mint on the one side, wafer biscuit on the other and top with one of the sauces of your fancy.

Toppings and Sauce	You will Require	Combining Method
Chocolate sauce	250 g chocolate 1 can evaporated milk 1 c sugar 1 t coffee	Melt chocolate in a double boiler over boiling water. Add sugar, cover and cook for 20 minutes. Add remaining ingredients. Beat until smooth and cook for 5 minutes. Serve hot over ice cream. Store in refrigerator for weeks.
Butterscotch sauce	1/2 c golden syrup 1/3 c butter 1 c brown sugar 1 c fresh cream	Cook syrup, butter and sugar until thickened for 15 minutes. Cool and add cream. Serve hot or cold.
Fudge nut sauce	1 c brown sugar 1 c white sugar 100 g chocolate 1/4 c cream 1 t vanilla essence 1/2 c chopped nuts	Cook over medium heat, sugar, chocolate and cream for 10 minutes. Cool, add nuts and vanilla essence.
Honey sauce	1/2 c honey 1/2 c cream 2 T butter	Mix and heat over low temperature for a few minutes. Serve warm.
Whipped cream topping	1 1/2 c cream 1/2 c sugar 1/4 t salt 1/2 t vanilla essence	Whip cream with sugar. Mix in seasoning and top on every Sundae.

Also delicious as a topping on two scoops of ice cream is the following:

Crushed tin pineapple
Sliced peaches
Orange segments
A spread of cherry, apricot or plum jam
1 T of honey with a sprinkling of nuts
Chopped bananas with brown sugar
1 T homemade marmalade
2 T chopped dates and honey
1 T maple syrup
A handful of chopped walnuts
A sprinkling of crushed coconuts biscuits with a touch of roasted coconut
Freshly shredded coconut
Melted chocolate
Grated chocolate
Chopped cherries
A sprinkling of drinking chocolate
Wafers and chopped marshmallows

A Variety of Ice Creams

Use one quantity of basic vanilla ice cream and combine with the following just before freezing.

Mango ice cream
Add the pulp of 3 large ripe mangoes.

Orange ice cream
Mix 250 (1 C) orange juice and 1 chopped orange with ice cream.

Strawberry ice cream
Puree 500 ml (2 C) strawberries, 60 ml (4 T) sugar and a drop of red colour in blender.

Lemon ice cream
Extract the juice of 2 lemons. Add the grated rind of 1 lemon and rind of 1 orange with lemon juice to ice cream.

Nutty Tutti Fruiti ice cream
Mix 500 ml (2 C) of glace fruit chopped finely to ice cream. Add 125 ml (1/2 c) walnuts, chopped coarsely.

Mocha ice cream
Mix 90 ml (6 T) instant coffee and 500 g of chocolate chips into ice cream.

Almond ice cream
Mix 500 ml (2 C) coarsely chopped almonds and 10 ml (2 t) almond essence. Use less essence in vanilla ice cream.

Banana ice cream
Mash ripe bananas. Blend into ice cream mixture. Drop a dash of yellow colour and blend well.

Saffron ice cream
Heat 2 ml (1/2 t) saffron strands in 45 ml (3 T) milk. Allow to steep and mix into ice cream.

Coconut ice cream
Place 500 ml (2 C) grated coconut in a pan in 180°C oven to roast until dry for 15 to 20 minutes. Mix into ice cream mixture before freezing.

Homemade chocolate cake, cookies and biscuits to make your outings more pleasant.

Eggless Cakes and Biscuits

Delightful sandwich cake
Chocolate cake
Crispy apple pie
Custard biscuits
Crunchies
Nankhatai
Snowballs
Softies
Viennese biscuits
Date and walnut loaf
Ginger biscuits
Spicy nut crescents
Walnut biscuits
Melting moments
Mocha biscuits
Date crisps
Fresh cream tarts
Jam slices

DELIGHTFUL SANDWICH CAKE

Serves 8 — Time : 1 hr 15 mins

62 ml (1/4 C) butter, at room temperature
250 ml (1 C) sugar
2 ml (1/2 t) vanilla essence
375 ml (1 1/2 C) flour, sifted
30 ml (2 T) custard powder, sifted
12 ml (2 1/2 t) baking powder, sifted
2 ml (1/2 t) salt
375 ml (1 1/2 C) milk (more if needed)
Grated rind of one lemon
125 ml (1/2 C) smooth apricot jam

Cream butter, sugar and essence together, adding the sugar gradually until fluffy and light.

Place grated lemon rind into butter and sugar mixture.

Combine the dry ingredients and mix into butter and sugar mixture gradually, adding milk alternatively to make soft mixture.

Beat for 5 minutes.

Place mixture into two cake tins.

Bake at 180°C for 35 to 40 minutes.

Allow to cool.

Use jam to sandwich together.

CHOCOLATE CAKE

Serves 8 — Time : 60 mins

375 ml (1 1/2 C) flour, sifted
10 ml (2 t) baking powder, sifted
62 ml (1/4 C) cocoa, sifted
A good pinch of salt
180 ml (3/4 C) sugar
45 ml (3 T) oil
250 ml (1 C) milk
5 ml (1 t) ground cinnamon
10 ml (2 t) grounded coffee mixed in 1 T water
200 g cooking chocolate
Cherries for decoration

Combine the flour, baking powder, cocoa, coffee, salt and cinnamon.

Put sugar in with dry ingredients.

Combine oil with milk and add to dry ingredients. Combine together well.

Cook in greased square loaf pan.

Bake for 40 to 45 minutes at 325 F (170°C).

Melt chocolate and pour over top of cool cake.

Top with cherries.

Note: Chocolate cannot be measured in cup. Weights have to be used for specific measurements especially for baking.

CRISPY APPLE PIE

| Serves 6 | Time : 60 mins |

45 ml (3 T) melted butter
60 g (1/2 C) caramel sugar
60 g (1/2 C) oats
65g (1/2 C) flour
45 ml (3 T) jam
5 ml (1 t) cinnamon powder
2 ml (1/2 t) ground cloves
Apple puree, sweetened (Boil 6 large apples with skins and 45 ml (3 T) sugar until soft)

Combine the melted butter, sugar, flour and oats.

Place in a baking pan and cook in a 180°C oven for 10 minutes.

Whilst cooking, stir the mixture a couple of times.

Cool.

Grease a shallow oven dish.

At the bottom of the dish spread the jam.

Place the apple puree and spices on top of the jam and crumble the oats mixture over the apple.

Bake in preheated oven at 180°C for 25 minutes.

CUSTARD BISCUITS

| Makes 75 | Time : 60 mins |

1000 ml (4 C) cake flour, sifted
250 ml (1 C) castor sugar
60 ml (4 T) custard powder
450 g (2 C) soft butter

Cream the butter and castor sugar together well.

Add the flour and custard powder and mix well.

Place dough into biscuit machine and make different biscuit designs.

Preheat oven to 180°C.

Bake on greased tray for 15 minutes.

CRUNCHIES

Makes 30   Time : 30 mins

125 ml (1/2 c) butter
30 ml (2 t) golden syrup
250 ml (1 c) bread flour
2 ml (1/2 t) bicarbonate of soda
2 ml (1/2 t) salt
500 ml (2 c) rolled oats
250 ml (1 c) grated coconut
200 ml (4/5 c) sugar
25 ml (5 t) milk

Melt the butter and add the syrup.

Sift the flour, bicarbonate of soda and salt together.

Add the rest of the ingredients and mix well.

Add to the melted butter and syrup mixture and mix well.

Press lightly and evenly into a greased pan and bake at 180°C for 15 to 20 minutes.

Cut into desired shapes.

Leave to cool for 10 to 15 minutes then remove from the pan.

Note: Golden syrup is bought already in a tin.

NAANKHATAI

Makes 40   Time : 60 mins

250 ml (1 C) sugar
250 ml (1 C) ghee
500 ml (2 C) cake flour, sifted
125 ml (1/2 C) chana flour, sifted
125 ml (1 1/2 C) semolina or Taystee wheat
5 ml (1 t) nutmeg and elaichi (cardamom seeds crushed)

Mix ghee and sugar.

Rub into flour.

Mix the dry ingredients into a dough.

If the dough is too soft add more flour.

Make the dough into small balls and bake on a greased baking sheet for 15 to 20 minutes at 180°C.

Remove from oven when slightly brown.

These traditional Indian biscuits are special.

SNOWBALLS

Makes 40   Time : 1 hr 15 mins

600 ml (2 2/5 c) flour
225 g (3/4 c) softened butter or margarine
40 ml (8 t) castor sugar
10 ml (2 t) vanilla essence
200 g (3/4 c) crushed nuts (hazelnuts or pecan nuts)
3/4 c icing sugar to roll biscuits in

Cream the butter and the sugar together well. Add the vanilla essence and the crushed nuts. Add the flour and mix together well.

Make small balls from the dough and place onto a baking sheet.

Bake for 40 to 45 minutes at 140°C.

When the balls have cooled roll them in icing sugar.

SOFTIES

Makes 75   Time : 60 mins

375 g (1 1/2 c) butter or margarine
375 ml (1 1/2 c) icing sugar
5 ml (1 t) vanilla essence
Pinch of salt
1125 ml (4 1/2 c) cake flour
Glace cherries for decoration

Cream the butter, sugar, vanilla essence and salt together. Add flour as required to make a soft mixture.

Place dough into a piping bag and pipe the dough into rosettes on a greased baking tray.

Decorate each with a glace cherry.

Bake at 180°C for 20 to 25 minutes.

VIENNESE BISCUITS

Makes 60   Time : 1hr 15 mins

225 g butter (3/4 c) butter
185 ml (3/4 c) castor sugar
750 ml (3 c) cake flour)
325 ml (1 1/2 c) coconut (freshly grated or dessicated)
2 ml (1/2 t) baking powder
30 ml (2 T) cocoa
100 g grated peppermint chocolate or
2 peppermint crisps

Cream butter and sugar very well.

Sift in the dry ingredients. Mix together well to form a dough.

Spread onto a greased tray and mark it with a fork all over.

Bake at 150°C for 40 to 45 minutes.

When removing from the oven, immediately sprinkle grated peppermint chocolate.

Cut into squares and cool.

DATE AND WALNUT LOAF

Cut 12 slices   Time : 1 hr 20 mins

250 ml (1 c) dates, chopped
250 ml (1 c) water
250 ml (1 c) sugar
60 ml (1/4 c) margarine or butter
250 ml (1 c) flour, sifted
5 ml (1 t) bicarbonate of soda
125 ml (1/2 c) chopped walnuts

Preheat oven to 150°C.

Combine dates, water, sugar and margarine in a saucepan. Stir over medium heat until sugar dissolves. Bring to a boil. Simmer for 4 minutes.

Allow to cool.

Stir in the flour, bicarbonate of soda and nuts.

Pour into greased loaf tin (220 mm x 120 mm).

Bake for 40 to 50 minutes.

GINGER BISCUITS

Makes 36　　Time : 60 mins

125 ml (1/2 c) soft butter or margarine
62 ml (1/4 c) golden syrup
62 ml (1/4 c) water
125 ml (1/2 t) bicarbonate of soda
500 ml (2 c) self raising flour
20 ml (4 t) ground ginger
185 ml (3/4 c) brown sugar

Melt the butter, golden syrup, water and bicarbonate of soda over low heat. Once melted allow to cool.
Sift dry ingredients.
Add to butter mixture. Stir well.
Roll into small balls and place on a greased baking sheet.
Press each ball with a fork.
Bake at 180°C for 10 to 15 minutes.

WALNUT BISCUITS

Makes 60　　Time : 60 mins

500 ml (2 c) margarine
375 ml (1 1/2 c) sugar, less if desired
750 ml (3 c) cake flour, sifted
250 ml (1 c) sesame seeds
500 ml (2 c) coconut (fine)
125 ml (1/2 c) chopped walnuts

Mix margarine and sugar.
Add the rest of the ingredients.
Shape into balls.
Place onto greased baking tray.
Bake at 150°C for 30 minutes.

SPICY NUT CRESCENTS

Makes 60　　Time : 65 mins

530 ml (2 1/8 c) cake flour
62 ml (1/4 c) maizena
2 ml (1/2 t) ground nutmeg
2 ml (1/2 t) ground cloves
190 ml (3/4 c) soft butter
125 ml (1/2 c) castor sugar
250 ml (1 c) ground almonds
Castor sugar for dipping biscuits

Mix butter and sugar together then add sifted flour and maizena, almonds, nutmeg and cloves.
Make into half moon shapes and place onto a greased baking tray.
Bake at 180°C until golden brown for about 20 minutes.
Remove from oven and immediately roll into castor sugar.

MELTING MOMENTS

Makes 36　　Time : 45 mins

250 ml (1 c) icing sugar
315 g (1 1/4 c) butter
Pinch of salt
250 ml (1 c) custard powder
310 ml (1 1/4 c) self raising powder

Cream butter and sugar. Add custard, salt and sifted flour. Bind into a dough.
Put dough in biscuit machine and make shapes. (Add more flour if dough is too soft).
Place on a greased pan and bake at 180°C (350°F) for 12 to 15 minutes.

Variations
This mixture can also be used in a biscuit machine to make fancy biscuits.

MOCHA BISCUITS

| Makes 48 | Time : 45 mins |

250 g butter (1 c) soft butter
175 g (1 1/2 c) sugar
625 ml (2 1/2 c) flour, sifted
7 ml (1 1/2 t) coffee granules
60 g (1 1/2 c) cocoa, sifted
15 ml (3 t) baking powder
2 ml (1/2 t) salt
1 T warm water
Chocolate nuggets for decoration

Mix butter and sugar together until creamy.

Place flour, cocoa, baking powder and salt with the butter and sugar mixture. Add 1 T t of warm water to coffee. Bind into dough.

Form little balls from the dough. Press a chocolate nugget on each ball.

Bake in 180°C oven for 12 minutes.

FRESH CREAM TARTS

| Makes 50 | Time : 60 mins |

4 c flour
4 t baking powder
250 g (1 c) soft butter
1 c fresh cream
100 g chocolate
62 ml (1/4 c) jam or 100 g seedless dates
Castor sugar for dipping

Sift the flour and baking powder together.

Add the butter and rub in until the mixture looks like bread crumbs. Add the cream to bind the mixture into a dough. Roll the dough out and cut into round shapes.

Place a piece of chocolate, a date or some jam onto the round and fold the dough round in half and seal the edges.

Bake for 15 to 20 minutes in preheated oven at 180°C.

Allow to cool and roll in castor sugar.

DATE CRISPS

| Makes 20 | Time : 45 mins |

1 1/2 packets marie biscuits*
250 g (1 c) soft butter or margarine
500 g (2 c) dates
250 ml (1 c) sugar
250 ml (1 c) dessicated coconut

Break biscuits into small pieces.

Melt dates, sugar and margarine in a large pot. Keep stirring to ensure it does not burn. Remove from heat when mixture is soft. Add biscuits.

Spread mixture in greased pan.

Place in fridge for a short while.

Cut into squares and sprinkle coconut over the squares.

   * Ginger biscuits can be used instead of marie biscuits but less sugar must then be used.

JAM SLICES

| Makes 24 | Time : 60 mins |

500 ml (2 c) flour
125 ml (1/2 c) castor sugar
250 g (1 c) margarine or butter
250 ml (1 c) smooth apricot jam – heat in microwave for 30 secs
62 ml (1/4 c) dessicated coconut

Cream margarine and sugar.

Add flour and bind dough together. Press down on greased baking tray.

Bake at 180°C for 20 to 25 minutes or until golden brown.

When baked spread with hot jam and sprinkle with coconut. Cut in squares.

An exquisitely hand carved papaya.

Fruit juice, punch, milkshake and sherbets

Saffron sherbet
Delicious rose milkshake
Indian fruit punch
Buttermilk sherbet – lassi
Fruit juice punch
Spicy tea – chai
Indian coffee

KESAR THANDAI – SAFFRON SHERBET

| Serves 4 | ⌚ Time : 40 mins |

1000 ml (4 c) milk
15 g (2 T) blanched almonds
15 g (2 T) pistachio nuts
5 ml (1 t) cardamom seeds
A few strands of saffron
30 ml (2 T) castor sugar
1 ml (1/4 t) grated nutmeg
1 ml (1/4 t) turmeric
Crushed ice

Grind almonds, nuts, cardamom, saffron, nutmeg and turmeric into a fine mixture using an electric coffee grinder.

Dissolve sugar in milk.

Mix all ingredients thoroughly and served chilled with crushed ice.

Thandai *or sherbets are special milk drinks, extremely popular over festive periods.*

Variations
Almond thandai

Use 50 g almonds, without pistachios in basic recipe.

Pista thandai

Use 50 g pistachio nuts without almonds in basic recipe.

Kesar thandai

Add 5 ml (1 t) of saffron powder to basic recipe.

DELICIOUS ROSE MILKSHAKE

| Serves 6 | ⌚ Time : 15 mins |

1000 ml (4 c) milk
500 ml (2 c) vanilla ice cream
10 ml (2 t) rose essence or
12 fresh rose petals, wash well and gently crush with fingertips to release aroma
15 ml (1 t) castor sugar

Mix ingredients in blender and serve chilled.

Variations
Instead of rose essence add the following :

Pista milkshake
Add 50 g ground pistachio nuts

Mango milkshake
Add the flesh of 1 ripe mango, 5 ml (1 t) crushed cumin

Orange milkshake
Add 15 ml (3 t) of grated orange rind or peel

Vanilla milkshake
Add 10 ml (2 t) vanilla essence

Raspberry milkshake
Add 10 ml (2 t) raspberry essence

Strawberry milkshake
Add 10 ml (2 t) strawberry essence

Chocolate milkshake
Add 10 ml (2 t) cocoa, 5 ml (1 t) good instant coffee

FRESH FRUIT SHERBET – INDIAN FRUIT PUNCH

| Serves 6 | Time : 25 mins |

1 litre (4 c) lemonade
60 g castor sugar
Juice of two lemons
250 ml (1 c) water
Grated rind of one lemon
1 banana peeled and sliced
1 apple peeled, quartered and thinly sliced
A few strawberries cut lengthwise in halves
A few grapes halved and pips removed
Mint leaves washed and chopped finely
1 orange with peel on, sliced and quartered
Pineapple, chopped
Crushed ice

Dissolve castor sugar in water.

Add lemonade, lemon juice and fruit. Mix well.

Serve chilled with crushed ice.

FRUIT JUICE PUNCH

| Serves 6 | Time : 15 mins |

1 litre (4 c) orange juice
250 ml (1 c) guava juice
10 ml (2 t) lemon juice
250 ml (1 c) cold black tea
500 ml (2 c) chopped fresh fruits (bananas, apples, pineapples, grapes)
15 ml (1 t) mint leaves, chopped
1000 ml (4 c) soda water

Mix present in a large punch bowl.

Serve in iced drinking glasses... see below.

How to prepare iced drinking glasses

Place 62 ml (1/4 c) sugar onto a plate. In another plate, add some water. Now, very carefully, wet just the edge of the glass, then dip into sugar and allow to dry. Pour punch into decorated glasses. Cut a thin round slice of lemon. Make a slit from the centre of the lemon round to the edge. Hang the lemon ring on the edge of the glass.

BUTTERMILK SHERBET – *LASSI*

| Serves 4 | Time : 15 mins |

500 ml (2 c) unsweetened yoghurt
45 ml (3 T) sugar (castor sugar if available)
2 ml (1/2 t) salt
150 ml water
Ice cubes
Grated lemon rind
Mint leaves

Beat yoghurt, sugar and salt until fluffy.

Add water and stir well.

Serve in tall glasses. Add ice and decorate with lemon rind and mint leaves.

Lassi, the excellent thirst quencher is consumed in large quantities because they replace the large loss of body water which occurs in India's tropical climate. Refreshing and nutritious, it is often drunk with meals.

Variations

Sweet *Lassi*

Add double quantity of sugar to basic recipe.

Kara *Lassi*

Remove sugar from basic recipe. Add 5 ml (1 t) freshly crushed black pepper and 5 ml (1 t) sugar.

Salt *Lassi*

Remove sugar from basic recipe. Add 10 ml (2 t) crushed cumin and 5 ml (1 t) sugar.

CHAI – SPICY TEA

| Serves 2 | Time : 10 mins |

375 ml (1 1/2 c) water
250 ml (1 c) milk
12 mm length of ginger, wash and pound
1 ml (1/4 t) tea masala, available at Indian stores, this masala is optional as it makes the tea spicy hot, or a pinch of pepper freshly ground
2 cardamom pods, partly split the pods
1 blade of citronella grass, cut into pieces
7 ml (1 1/2 t) tea leaves
20 ml (4 t) sugar, less may be added for health reasons, may be sweetened with non-saccharine vegetable sweetener

Place the water into a deep saucepan.

Add the milk and bring to the boil.

The milk and water has to be watched constantly as it will boil over.

Add the ginger, tea masala, cardamom pods and citronella grass and simmer gently on a medium heat for 2 minutes.

Add the tea leaves and stir in the sugar.

Bring the mixture to boil and then simmer for a few minutes until the tea turns a caramel colour.

Remove from heat and strain tea into a teapot.

Tea is poured directly into tea cups in the Indian kitchen before it is served to guests. Savouries are served with tea in the usual manner.

An Indian tea preparation – one of the finest teas in the world, guaranteed to take away a headache or cold. Indians drink this tea throughout the day more as a nourishing drink than just as a refresher.

Tea leaves are boiled with milk and water, then flavoured with spices such as cardamom, pepper and cinnamon. Citronella grass which is a sweet smelling blade of grass, is also used as an added flavouring and freshly pounded ginger just gives the cup that characteristic taste.

Tea without the spices is also flavoursome due to the vanilla flavour.

INDIAN COFFEE

| Serves 2 | Time : 10 mins |

500 ml (2 c) water
250 ml (1 c) milk
12 ml (2 1/2 t) freshly ground coffee beans
20 ml (4 t) sugar
5 ml (1 t) cardamom seeds

Bring water and milk to the boil.

Add sugar, coffee and cardamom and simmer, for 10 minutes, until strong.

Strain and serve in stainless steel cups.